*Test...*

The common thread that weaves its way through the fabric of the pages in *Budding Romance for Late Bloomers* is faith – faith in a higher power and the voice that speaks from within, and having the self-confidence to listen, to wait until the heart yells, "Yes!" Fox has compiled an excellent read for any man or woman. Most likely you will say, "She's talking about me."

Susan Parker, Writer and Poet

Maureen has spilled her heart and will inevitably help you to find more of yours and make choices that more closely reflect it. And that's the most we can hope for … or offer the man of our dreams!

Jan Denise, author of *Naked Relationships* and *Innately Good*, founder of Godseed Originals

Maureen Fox's witty, provocative book, *Budding Romance for Late Bloomers*, inspires with vignettes of love found after forty. Her creativity and spiritual insights give hope to those who still want to experience a loving relationship. Guidance for dating offers sound advice, expressed in a voice that feels professional, yet personal. You will smile as you read the stories of the women who shared their experiences as their love blossomed.

Karen Souther, friend

# Budding Romance
## for Late Bloomers

Women's first marriages over 40, 50, 60

Maureen Candace Fox

Order this book online at www.trafford.com
or email orders@trafford.com

Most Trafford titles are also available at major online book retailers.

Some of the names contained in this book have been changed to protect the privacy of the
individuals. Some of the stories I gathered by placing advertisements in the newspaper the
year after I got married in 1996. More recent stories I obtained via word of mouth—some
sent in their stories and I edited, others I interviewed and submitted my final copy for
their approval, and a few "in their own words." All individuals whose stories are contained
herein were advised at the time that I was gathering stories for a book I was hoping
to get published. They were only too willing to be part of such an undertaking.

Printed in the United States of America.

ISBN: 978-1-4669-1508-4 (sc)
ISBN: 978-1-4669-1510-7 (hc)
ISBN: 978-1-4669-1509-1 (e)

Library of Congress Control Number: 2012902700

*Trafford rev. 03/14/2012*

 www.trafford.com

North America & international
toll-free: 1 888 232 4444 (USA & Canada)
phone: 250 383 6864 ♦ fax: 812 355 4082

This book is lovingly dedicated to the memory of my mother, Eve Erskine, who enjoyed writing and who would have been extremely proud to know I followed in her footsteps.

# Acknowledgments

I am eternally grateful to all my close friends who were most supportive of my idea for this book, right from the start. Their belief in me and my intention has never wavered. I would like to acknowledge a few special people who stand out, mainly for their enthusiasm, their feedback, and their moral support: my forever friend, Sue Lennox, for planting the seed and sending information on self-publishing; dear friends Karen Souther, Sue Parker, and author Jan Denise, for agreeing to read my manuscript and offer feedback; Dianne Wilcoxon, who also provided feedback after reading my manuscript and was my researcher extraordinaire; the Dream Divas—Debbi Allen, Lottie Luse, Kim Licon, and Pam Waxlax, who provide their love and support each month as we set our intentions and celebrate our achievements, and past co-workers Marilynn Yeates, Jan Lane and Sherion Pagan whose whatever-we-can-do support and enthusiasm are soul enriching at our catch-up dinners. I would like to thank all the courageous and wonderful women who willingly agreed to share their beautiful love stories in this book. I can't forget my sister, Liz Walker, who always has been my greatest fan and my usual cohort in my other projects (she calls them my "cockamamie schemes"), and my brother, Mort Erskine, whose support I feel by his quiet strength and his willingness to listen. Last but certainly not least, my cherished friends Joan and Wayne Wutzke, for encouraging me to "run with it" (they know I don't do broke well) and for taking the photo of me for this book.

# Preface

This book is a shining light to all women who have loved, who have lost, and who have given up on ever finding love again.

I started writing this book many years ago, when I was newly married and still had my head in the clouds. I recount my journey to love and marriage at age fifty-three, along with other women over forty, fifty, and sixty who candidly share their secrets for letting go of their safely guarded independence to take another chance on love; the barriers they overcame; the circumstances that prevailed and their willingness to adapt; new perceptions and attitudes adopted; and fate that intervened, turning their dreams into realities. I gleaned snippets of information from the experts in the field of relationships, capturing the essence of love's most important lessons.

We know that we cannot change our past but what about our future? The stories contained herein will prove that love can happen when we have that burning desire to persist and make it happen, and in some cases, when we completely let go and focus on our passion, determining what it is we really want and need to make us happy.

The best is yet to come!

# Contents

## PART I

Love Stories: Women's First Marriages over 40, 50, 60 . . .

## PART II

Getting Back In The Game

# *Introduction*

This book was prompted by my friends' reaction to my marriage at age fifty-three. Their exuberance, joy, and genuine expressions of love were heartwarming. After their spirited congratulations, they drilled me with questions: "How did you meet him?" "Where did you meet him?" "What did you do differently?" They acted like it was a mystical experience or some kind of phenomenon. Their enthusiasm and energy would have kept the Energizer Bunny going until the next millennium. The news of my marriage quickly spread throughout my social network like a grass fire. Those of similar age and still single were unmistakably moved, claiming I had given them hope that they, too, would find a mate and marry one day. And some of them did.

It didn't dawn on me until six months into my marriage how beneficial it would be for other single women to read about older women who waited until after age forty, fifty, and even sixty to meet their mates and to learn that it is not impossible—that it is even probable—for those who desire it and even to those who have given up hope. I thought a book detailing other women's journeys to love would be inspirational, supportive, and reassuring—to know that a perfect mate can be found without having to compromise or settle for second best. I want to dispel the myth that "women over forty have a better chance of getting captured by aliens than getting married."

This book contains stories of women who waited until after the age of forty to get married for the first time, except for one story of a second marriage that I had to include because it is truly magical. Each has her own interesting and unique story. You'll discover why some waited so long to marry, why some were determined never to risk falling in love again, the lessons they learned, and the obstacles they overcame. You'll learn if it was fate that intervened, if it was love at first sight, or if a friendship developed over time and blossomed into a full-blown, lasting love affair.

I'm sure most single women would agree: it is not easy being single when you are over forty. Society still believes there must be something wrong with you; otherwise, why would a nice woman like you still be single?

Most women over forty and still single have had at least one opportunity to marry, contrary to what others might think. We chose a different path, one that provided many different experiences than for those who married in their twenties and thirties. I'm sure that if I had married at a younger age, I would have gone through two or three marriages by now. I was definitely not ready at thirty. Judging from today's statistics, the high divorce rate confirms this statement. In my case, I had a lot to learn about myself and about relationships. I learned that if you have confusion or resistance about anything, it will keep manifesting in your life until you resolve it; hence, my long journey to love and marriage.

Society's perception of the older single woman is slowly changing. They readily accept the choices she makes, whether she chooses to remain single, to be a career woman, a single mother, or whatever she wants. The field is wide open. It's all about making the right choice for you. It certainly takes the pressure off.

One time, I ran into an old classmate during intermission at a tennis match, a man I hadn't seen in over a decade. After hearing I was still single, he blurted out, "You're not gay, are you?" I almost choked on my hot dog. Maybe he would have choked on his, had I said yes. "Not that there's anything wrong with that." As heard on *Seinfeld* television show. Most single women will agree that it is a major struggle to protect one's self-image and maintain one's self-worth during those lonely times when the men are scarce and the future looks bleak.

What about all those well-meaning family and friends who think we are too picky, too selfish, too independent, too fickle, and too noncommittal. It makes me think of something I once read: "If you wait too long for your knight in shining armor, you'll find yourself cleaning up after the horse."

# PART I

## Love Stories:
### Women's First Marriages over 40, 50, 60 . . .

## *My story: Maureen and David*

I thought single life was great . . . in my teens, twenties, and thirties. I just never expected it to continue on into my forties and . . . er . . . um . . . fifties. I had a chronic case of the grass-is-always-greener syndrome. I had lots of opportunities to get married, starting from the age of sixteen, but always found reasons why it wasn't the right person or the right time.

Throughout my life, my intuition always has guided me. I was not fully aware of this at the time, but my inner sense kept me from marrying when I was younger and kept me from marrying the wrong person. I didn't always understand why I was saying no when part of me was screaming yes, but in looking back as well as knowing some of these men today, I'm glad my inner sense was the stronger voice.

Throughout my dating years, I questioned why I could not develop deeper feelings for certain men—the nice ones with whom I felt totally comfortable and felt free to be me. Many times, I tried to get past those platonic feelings (love from the neck up) without much success. Finally, I had a powerful insight that changed my perception. It was like a flash from the universe. I learned that the reason I was not attracted to certain men was because there was nothing I could learn from them.

On the other hand, whenever I had a strong, magnetic attraction to someone, I learned the most powerful lessons from him and gained the most insight into myself, like it or not.

Briefly, starting from the age of sixteen, I had my first crush, which lasted, intermittently, long into my twenties. I probably would have married him then, but he didn't ask. Years later, after I moved on to the big city of Vancouver, he came back into my life to propose to me in my mid-twenties, then again in my forties. Although, he still made my heart race, I was not as starry-eyed and was keenly aware I would be much happier staying single than adapting to his reckless lifestyle.

Another romance I had in my teens was with the first man (he was twenty-two) who told me he loved me. Although he was only in my life a short time, he made an impact. When he suggested we get married, I got scared and determined that I was far too young and needed to experience more of the world. (My inner guide provided me with an easy way out, although looking back, I sometimes wonder, "What if.")

In my early twenties, I was introduced to a very cool guy, on a blind date, arranged by a mutual friend of ours. The chemistry was certainly going on, but when he spontaneously asked me to get engaged, I panicked. I think there was too much going on in my life at the time—I wasn't ready. Are you seeing a pattern here?

At twenty-seven, I actually made a commitment to a man who I had lived with for over a year. I thought we would eventually marry, but our trip to Australia opened my eyes, and once home again, our relationship was never the same.

In my thirties, I had a noncommittal relationship with an interesting and fun man, but he was involved with too many other women. Too many squaws in his teepee, as my friend, Sue, would say. This led up to a final disastrous affair at age forty-two, which turned out to be a blessing.

In 1995, I had a challenging job, working for the president and CEO of a high-technology firm. I was financially secure, had many close friends, and led a physically active and healthy lifestyle—I was happy and content with myself and with my life. In the spring of that year, I decided to take a vacation. A friend's photographs convinced me that Cabo San Lucas looked like a fun place to visit.

It wasn't until my friend, Julie, and I were thirty thousand feet in the air and well on our way to our vacation destination that I recalled what Gloria Brough, a Vancouver psychic, had predicted for me the previous year: "It looks like you will be taking a trip south; it looks like Mexico." (At the time, my focus had been on Hawaii.) "It will be the right time and the right place," she'd said. (I didn't know what she meant by this, but I was about to find out.) She continued with her prediction: she saw me getting married in a beautiful garden in the presence of one hundred guests. My husband would have two full-grown sons, and she saw me living in a warm climate in the United States. When she finished my reading that day, Gloria had said, "You know, I'm also an ordained minister; I could marry you." I laughed it off with, "I'll keep that in mind." I never believed for a minute that I would be calling her the next year, asking her to perform my marriage ceremony.

The first day in Cabo San Lucas was spent shopping and familiarizing ourselves with our surroundings near the Plaza Las Glorias Hotel. By late afternoon, Julie and I ended up at Salsitas, an outside café hugging the marina, near the town center. As we were about to sit down at a table, the most amazing thing happened. I was about to say, "Let's sit over there," pointing to a table on the opposite side of the café, when a loud voice inside my head stopped me in my tracks: "Just sit down." So I did. How could I argue? As I gazed at the activity in the harbor, my friend chatted to the people seated at the next table. When I turned to see with whom she was talking, my eyes came to rest on an extremely attractive man. He was wearing a panama hat, sunglasses, and the sexiest smile I could have imagined. My heart reacted immediately, like an electric shock. He introduced himself as David, and then he introduced his son, Tai, and his stepson, Chris. They were on a week's vacation from Tacoma, Washington. We talked easily for a while, and I found myself eagerly agreeing to join him on the golf course the next day. After golf, I accepted his invitation to lunch at Las Palmilla, an ultra-lush resort filled with a romantic ambiance. The very next day (I later learned), David told his brother, "I think I have met 'the one.'" This was the beginning of our incredible love story.

David's situation was more complicated than mine: He was a single parent and was currently involved with someone, but assured me it wasn't "a Dr. Zhivago-and-Lara type relationship."

The entire week was like a dream, with each day more exciting than the one before. We eagerly awaited each new day, when we would be together again. It was a sensual, intoxicating experience, making it difficult to keep our emotions in check. I felt more comfortable, however, with keeping our relationship on a platonic level until David's relationship situation changed. David agreed wholeheartedly, not wanting to put me in a position that I "did not deserve" (his words). It was hard to believe that such a man existed. I was completely charmed by his integrity, humor, intellect, compassion, and style.

After an unforgettable week of dining, snorkeling, laughing, golfing, and spending time with his family, we said good-bye. David left me with a promise: "I don't know how long it will take, but I will end my relationship as soon as humanly possible."

I spent another week in Cabo San Lucas before heading home and back to work—and to reality. The second week was not nearly as much fun as the first, although I did meet another nice man, more than comfortably rich, who took me out for dinner and gave me a tour of his yacht, which was moored at the marina near the Plaza Las Glorias. Our relationship might have been different, had I not already fallen head over heels for David. My feelings for him overpowered any I might have felt for this very nice man.

Returning to work on Monday was beyond exciting. Coworkers gathered to hear the tales of my romantic adventure. Later in the day, the receptionist called my office to say I had received flowers. I flew down three flights of stairs to Reception and ripped open the card that accompanied the bouquet, which read: "Here's to sidewalk cafés, panama hats, sun visors, and shades. Welcome back."

And that wasn't all! When I arrived home that evening, a love letter from David came by mail, reassuring me that the promise he had made to me in Cabo was still intact. What a marvelous gift!

True to his word, a month later David arrived on my doorstep. The minute I opened the door, I instinctively knew he was the man I had been waiting for all these years. We spent a wonderful weekend together, and before he left on Sunday, he professed his love for me.

The day after he arrived home, he called with the long-awaited news; he had ended his relationship with his lady friend, and he and Tai had moved into an apartment. It wasn't until the following weekend, when we met at his sister's place, halfway between our two cities, that we celebrated our relationship. He was well worth the wait.

On a beautiful night in June, in a courtyard setting at Il Giardino restaurant in Vancouver, David casually proposed marriage, although, it wasn't until that fall that David bought the engagement ring. We were vacationing in Palm Desert.

9

Both of us were ill with some kind of flu bug, and we were on our way to find a health food store at the local shopping mall. This was not a planned event—it was totally spur of the moment. You might say, "A funny thing happened on the way to the health food store." While we were walking past Hatfield Jewelers at the mall, we couldn't help but be drawn inside. A huge celebration was taking place. Colorful balloons filled the store, champagne was flowing, and the store was packed with happy people. Before I knew it, we were standing in front of a display of engagement rings, and I was trying one on. David said, "We might as well, we're going to do it sooner or later." I was so excited, I'm sure I chose the first ring I tried on—it was beautiful.

We chose the following June for a romantic outdoor wedding, against a backdrop of colorful flowers, at Peace Arch Park, located at the Canada/United States border, in the presence of one hundred guests. It was by far the most exciting day of my life. A few years ago, no one could have convinced me that this day would become a reality. To marry a man I truly loved—and who loved me back—was inconceivable. It proved one thing. Dreams do come true, and miracles do happen—and they don't always happen to someone else.

*It is a funny thing about life:*
*if you refuse to accept anything but the best,*
*you very often get it.*

—Somerset Maugham

## *Hannah and Senator Wynick*

When Hannah was in her forties, she was busily involved with her career when she first met her mate. At the time, he was a senator, married, and the father of two children.

Hannah's position as president of a library association and library lobbyist brought her in front of Senator Wynick, who at the time was Chairman of The Higher Education and Libraries Committee. Being the only professional librarian nearest his district, she would drive to the small town where he lived to meet with him. He always played the perfect host, taking her to upscale restaurants in the better part of town for dinner.

The senator's wife and children lived in a nearby city so that their children could attend a private Catholic school there. The only other personal fact Hannah knew about the senator was relayed to her by one of his close friends, who said, "The senator is a very unhappy man." Five years later, a notice of Senator Wynick's divorce appeared in the local newspaper. When Hannah's secretary brought it to her attention, it was news to her; he had never mentioned a word about this.

On the last day of the legislative session, which was always chaotic, the state librarian sent Hannah to check on the status of a very important appropriation for library development. Because this was a new federal initiative, it was critical to balance the national and state financial figures. Hannah's mission: to determine whether there was money in the budget for libraries.

Senator Wynick sat on the consequential conference committee responsible for making the final spending decisions. When Hannah first approached him to request money, he responded, "No. Library money was cut out. Ask Senator Blake, the other chairman." When Hannah asked Senator Blake, he blew up in a fury, demanding, "Where are you from? Ah, I know who told you to ask me." He pushed past her and stormed onto the floor of the Senate, shouting at the top of his lungs at Senator Wynick. Senator Wynick, red-faced, head lowered like an angry bull, strode off the Senate floor, heading in Hannah's direction. He unleashed his anger at her, grunting, "Go back home until you've learned more about the rules of legislature!" Through this experience, Hannah understood that she was supposed to beg for money without revealing her knowledge that it had been eliminated altogether.

Back home that evening, Hannah immediately scribbled a note of apology to Senator Wynick. Simultaneously, Senator Wynick did the same.

Hannah maintains to this day, "Knowing how your future husband looks and behaves when he is in a total fury is good practice for marriage."

Senator Wynick's courtship was extremely casual. He often stopped by Hannah's to take her to dinner on his way to visit his daughters in the city. Sometimes he was alone, sometimes he had a daughter with him, or sometimes he had his huge Newfoundland dog. Once, he even had a piano tossed in the back of his decrepit pickup truck.

When Hannah was struck by a serious attack of malignant hypertension, forcing her into the hospital for three weeks, Senator Wynick chose this time to propose marriage. He burst into her room, blurting out, "As soon as you are better, we are going to get married. I'm going to send you off to my summer retreat to speed up your recovery."

They were married that fall, with only their attendants and his big black Newfoundland dog as witnesses.

Hannah found the transition of leaving a challenging job to tend house extremely difficult, especially in a town she immensely disliked. It was a nowhere town, with not much to do and very few good restaurants. Adding to her stress was the task of developing a friendship with her two new stepdaughters, which was no small feat. Nevertheless, she claims, it was all worth it. She maintains that their marriage partnership is perfect. They laugh at the same jokes, they read the same books, and they have similar friendships. They enjoy doing the same things, which includes great sex, and as they look forward to their thirtieth wedding anniversary, they still are madly in love.

Hannah confirms, "I'm so glad I waited until the absolutely right partner came into my life. I've seen so many teens and those in their twenties, whose marriages fail. They are led by their glands into disastrous, unsatisfying relationships, resulting in divorces and dysfunctional offspring." She emphatically believes women should wait until they are older to marry—so much so that she has issued a warning to her niece, whose college tuition she is funding: "If you get married while you're still in college, the funding will immediately stop, and you will not receive the rest of your inheritance until you turn twenty-seven."

Hannah claims it was her interesting and all-consuming career that kept her from marrying at a younger age, although her family believes it was because she was "too picky."

The senator was the only man who stole her heart. Previous friendships with men never ripened into anything deeper; they remained just friends.

Her only regret is not having children, although today, she feels like a mother in every sense of the word, except genetically. She brags about her four great-grandchildren.

She would not change a thing. She feels blessed to have found a mate with whom she is so perfectly suited.

*While faith makes all things possible,*
*love makes all things beautiful.*

—unknown

# *Brenda and Steve*

Brenda and I met some twenty-five years ago, when we were dating two men who hung around in the same crowd. Brenda and I soon became good friends and compatible travel partners. We took many memorable ski vacations together.

On one of our getaways, Brenda met a man from California who she liked a lot. They continued their long-distance romance for a few years, until one day he ended it abruptly. She was justifiably shattered. It wasn't long after that when she got caught up in an affair with her boss, a married man. At the beginning, their relationship was light and easy and fun, but it soon transformed into one of control and obsession. She felt her only escape route was to accept a job in another city.

When Brenda returned several years later, she was self-composed, serene, and eager to jump back into the dating scene. Years passed, however, without anyone stealing her heart—or even causing it to flutter. At times, she would get so disheartened and frustrated with the dating situation, she preferred to stay at home watching television.

I remember well the first time Brenda met Steve. I had to drag her, kicking and screaming, to a local restaurant. It was a month past her forty-eighth birthday. I had promised to take her out for dinner, but she was reluctant to go, claiming she did not feel good about herself. Finally, after much persuasion, she consented to join me for dinner at a local hotel.

After dinner, I talked her into having a nightcap at the adjoining disco. We had one drink and then left. We were not in the mood for disco music but discovered another bar with a live band at the other end of the hotel. No sooner had we sat down than a pleasant-looking, silver-haired man with a young face approached our table. He said his name was Steve, and he asked me to dance. We had one dance, and then he asked Brenda for the next dance. He held Brenda captive on the dance floor for the rest of the evening.

Brenda was thrilled when Steve asked her for a date the next day. She played it safe by suggesting they go for a walk. She decided if she didn't like him, she could excuse herself early without hurting his feelings.

I called Brenda the next week and heard the good news—she and Steve had been out on a few dates since their Sunday walk; in fact, he was calling her on a regular basis. I knew their relationship was serious when Brenda invited Steve to spend Christmas with her family. In my twenty-five years of knowing her, no man had ever been granted that privilege.

After Christmas, Brenda and Steve flew to Mexico for two weeks. This was the real test—if they could make it through a two-week vacation together, then it must be the real thing. As it turned out, it was. The following year they returned to Mazatlan. This time, Steve proposed marriage to Brenda.

Although there had been a few blips in their relationship along the way, they flew off to Reno, Nevada, to marry in Brenda's forty-ninth year.

When Brenda met Steve, the timing was obviously right. She was open and receptive to accepting a special person in her life. You see, Brenda had been a workaholic and very disciplined. She worked long into the night and often on weekends, while her friends gadded about; her work regimen left little time for her to meet anyone. As it turned out, when she met Steve, she recently had left her job and was trying to get a home business off the ground. You might say she was ripe for the picking. Leaving secure employment was a huge leap out of her comfort zone, making her more vulnerable.

*You've got to have a dream if you want it to come true.*

—Dr. Denis Waitley, *The Psychology of Winning*

## *Donna and Russ*

Donna's long journey to love was no fluke. It happened through intense self-examination, reading books, and diligently setting out to define what she wanted and needed in a partner.

Donna had been in and out of many different relationships since the age of twenty. She'd had several long-term relationships with live-in partners, the longest one lasting six years. She was a free spirit, independent, and artistic—a spiritually inclined wild child who chose practical, stable, conservative, and uptight partners. Their initial fascination with each other quickly transformed into a power struggle when each tried molding the other into a more acceptable form.

In 1989, after ending an unhealthy, confidence-busting, three-year live-in relationship, Donna turned within, focusing on her interests and dating only occasionally.

In 1992, Donna decided to expand her social circle and accepted an invitation to a friend's party. At this party, she met a gorgeous, successful, unique man, with whom she shared an immediate dynamic chemistry. This relationship turned out to be the catalyst to getting the love she really wanted. Over the next three months, this man labored to win her love, but just as their relationship began heating up, he abruptly broke it off on New Year's Eve.

January 1, 1993, found Donna languishing in a La-Z-Boy chair, fighting the flu, and feeling devastated over this recent breakup. Overcome with despair, she turned to her friends for comfort and support. She was hoping they would distract her and get her through the next couple of weeks. When her shakiness subsided, she started dating again in an effort to erase her most recent partner from her mind. She placed a personal ad in the *Seattle Weekly* newspaper—a girlfriend had met her current beau through the personal ads, Donna reasoned, so why shouldn't she try it? Out of 120 respondents, she met with forty and then selected three or four she found suitable to date. This was a major learning experience that had a dual purpose: she learned what she really wanted in a partner, and it was a boost to her fragile ego. She made lots of notes as she went through the dating process, refining her "recipe" for Mr. Right.

In late May, something shifted in Donna's mind-set, and she realized the men she'd been dating failed to meet her expectations. They each had a piece of the puzzle, but not one of them had it all. She wanted a partner who shared her values; someone who accepted her and appreciated her; someone who supported her; someone who was crazy about her; and someone who was willing to put himself on the line for her. He had to be the total package.

For a long time, Donna suspected that she might not be destined to marry or that she would have to make huge sacrifices or compromise in order to have a partner.

After reading a book on soul mates, Donna believed that if God created her, then surely he created a suitable mate for her as well. Another book, this one on "treasure mapping," taught her to be specific about what she really wanted and not to be distracted by lesser offers. She learned to wait for clues (treasures) that came her way. A "clue" can be described as an aspect or part of what one desires, whereas a "treasure" is the most valuable, it contains everything one wants and more. These clues met some of her criteria but were missing key elements. This proved, however, that the universe was working on her request. If she accepted a clue as her treasure, then that's all she would receive. If she held out for what she really wanted, then the universe would send further clues her way until her treasure finally arrived.

After coming to this understanding, Donna decided to end all her current connections. She was through accepting "clues"; she was ready for the real treasure. She found she didn't need a man in her life. She enjoyed her own company and that of friends. She was through wasting energy on relationships that didn't nurture and support her.

Shortly thereafter, while attending a singles event, Donna won a free personal advertisement in the *Seattle Weekly* newspaper. Her future husband, Russ, replied to her ad.

Donna met Russ when she had clearly decided not to sell herself short in relationships and when she had committed herself to living a joyful life, whether she got married or stayed single.

When Donna and Russ first met, she says, "The earth did not move. I was pleased with his looks, his history was compatible with mine, and he fit most of my immediate criteria." She said their first meeting was more of an interview; Russ remembers it as an interrogation. At the time, Donna was so busy that she had little time to date. Russ, however, kept creeping into her thoughts. While on a six-week retreat, Donna mused that maybe she would start dating Russ when she returned. Maybe he would be "the one"—and maybe they would get married and live happily ever after.

Donna returned home from the retreat to find several messages from Russ on her answering machine. A family crisis prevented her from returning his calls right away—her father was facing major heart surgery.

Right from the start, Russ did everything right. He followed her recipe for Mr. Right to a T. She says, "It was uncanny." Of course, he knew nothing of her long, detailed list.

Because Donna was under a great deal of emotional stress due to her father's health crisis, she moved cautiously into her new relationship with Russ. Luckily, Russ was extremely patient and understanding—and persistent. By November, she was madly in love with him.

Hindsight told Donna that being so immersed in her family crisis actually served her in developing a relationship with Russ. She did not have the energy to keep up her usual walls and protections, nor did she care to do so. She kept everything up front—no games, no approval seeking. She adopted the attitude, "This is me; take it or leave it." He took it! He loved Donna for who she was. Donna says, "This has been one of the most profoundly healing experiences in my life. It is incredibly wonderful to be fully seen, appreciated, loved, and supported." This relationship made all her past relationships look incredibly foolish. With Russ, she found a relationship that not only met all her requirements but offered the kind of love beyond anything she had ever envisioned for herself. It was unlike any she had previously experienced. In the past, Donna made few demands of her partner and had few expectations. This was consistent with her belief that no one would accept her as she was. She believed she was too picky, too unrealistic, and too weird, and she believed she would have to change substantially in order to have someone in her life.

Donna's path to love entailed years of poor choices, difficult lessons, and a lot of self-examination. She wrote out in detail the characteristics she wanted and didn't want in a mate, and then she committed herself to accepting only the best. From there, she took deliberate action in search of someone who fit her description for a mate. Ironically, it was only after Donna put this aside and got caught up in another aspect of her life—her father's illness—that her dream man appeared. Her attention was on something and someone other than herself. This tells me that it is necessary to set goals and be specific about them, but then let them go so they can gather the energy needed to bring them to fruition. I've heard it described as "getting out of your own way."

After years of marriage, Donna and Russ are still deeply in love. They are comfortably compatible; they enjoy each other's company; they have mutual respect; and they bring out the best in each other. Donna says, "We are deeply grateful for the grace of God that ultimately brought us together. It is never too late to find the blessings of love. Some of us just take longer to get there."

*He who trims himself to suit everybody*
*will soon whittle himself away.*

—Laurence J. Peter, *The Peter Prescription*

## *Bernice and Ronald*

Bernice and Ronald met in March 1974, two months after her fortieth birthday. Their meeting had been foretold some months earlier by a tea-cup reader. She predicted Bernice would attend a social gathering—possibly an anniversary of some sort—and would meet someone who was very interested in her. The reader also saw two gold rings. Bernice was a bit of a skeptic, not putting much credence in this sort of thing.

Bernice worked as a registered nurse on the maternity ward in Brantford, a small town in southern Ontario, Canada, where she'd lived all her life. After her parents died, she moved to an upstairs apartment in a house within walking distance to the hospital. A kind elderly couple, Will and Annie Ronald, lived downstairs.

In March, the Ronalds invited Bernice to attend their sixtieth wedding anniversary celebration. Shy and reserved, Bernice reluctantly accepted—she didn't want to disappoint Mrs. Ronald. While standing in the reception line, waiting to offer her congratulations, Bernice was introduced to the Ronalds' nephew, Ronald Simpson, a farmer from Manitoba. They briefly chatted before Bernice escaped to her apartment upstairs.

Two days later, Ronald called to say he would like a chance to get to know Bernice. He was returning home the next day and asked if he could write to her. When Ronald's letter arrived, Bernice read it—and then reread it at least five or six times before responding. After that, letters flew back and forth, and Ron's telephone bills escalated.

Through his letters, Bernice learned that Ron was forty-nine years old and had been farming since high school. He lived with his parents, then in their eighties, in a little village called Brookdale, 120 miles west of Winnipeg. He was an only son, with a younger sister who was married and lived on a nearby farm.

Ron finally got around to asking Bernice to spend her summer vacation with him in Manitoba. He assured her that she had his parents' blessing and would be staying with them. Bernice jumped at the opportunity to revisit that part of the country, having toured the Prairies the previous year.

Early in July, Ron picked Bernice up in Winnipeg, and they drove on to Brookdale. As they spent time touring the farm and other places he mentioned in his letters, their friendship grew. On July 18, four months after meeting, Ron proposed, and Bernice said yes. She was naive and innocent and inexperienced with men, but she thought he was the nicest, most decent man she had ever met.

Returning to work sporting a big diamond ring, Bernice caused quite a stir. Everyone was flabbergasted. They couldn't believe that quiet, shy Bernice had found herself a mate. Ron and Bernice exchanged their vows in a small Brookdale church on November 9, 1974.

The one thing missing in the Simpsons' marriage was children. They both dearly loved children and were eager to start a family right away. With this in mind, Ron built a new three-bedroom house on the farm. In 1975, Bernice consulted an obstetrician/gynecologist, who was confident Bernice could conceive, despite her age. Unfortunately, her hopes of conceiving were dashed when an examination revealed uterine fibroids. A hysterectomy was inevitable.

The Simpsons both agreed that adoption was an option and immediately contacted the Children's Aid Society. They didn't qualify for adoption of a baby or toddler because of their older age, so they agreed to accept a child under ten. They even agreed to take more than one child, if that would improve their chances.

In the spring of 1977, the call came from Children's Aid Society. They had two children available: a brother and a sister of Irish-Danish origin. Bernice and Ron were ecstatic. They rushed over to meet Charlie and Sharon, six-year-old twins who had been in foster care for the past two years. They had been taken away from their birth parents because of repeated neglect. When Bernice and Ron expressed interest in the twins, Mrs. Hill, the social worker, explained there was another sister, three-and-a-half-year-old Irene, who also was available for adoption. Hesitantly, Mrs. Hill asked, "Would you consider taking all three to keep the family together?" The answer was a resounding yes. Bernice and Ron were overjoyed; it all seemed too good to be true. Early in June 1977, Bernice and Ron traveled four hundred miles to pick up the children and introduce them to their new home.

The first few weeks were extremely hectic. Mrs. Hill regularly dropped in to see how Bernice and Ron were managing. Even she was astonished at the children's wild and unruly behavior. She reassured Bernice that the children were "testing" them. The children consistently quarreled and tormented one another and were jealous and possessive of anything they considered theirs, including their chairs at the kitchen table. They were suspicious of each other, of their new parents, and of any change to their normal routine. Often, by the end of the day, Bernice would fall into bed, exhausted.

Before they were adopted, the children had been told about their new parents and their new home. At the time, Bernice wondered how much they had absorbed, especially little Irene. Her background differed from the twins. The twins had been in the same foster home for two years, from age four to six. Irene was only eighteen months old when she was put into foster care and had lived with three different families, eleven months with the last one. During this time, Irene rarely saw her brother and sister.

After her first few weeks on the farm, Irene kept talking about going home. On laundry day, Irene would point to her clean clothes and say, "I'm going to put these in my suitcase and go home." Bernice would counter, "You are home. This is your home." One day while Bernice was holding her, Irene suddenly looked up at her, eyes as big as saucers, as if she had a sudden dawning, and said, "Are you the new mommy and daddy?" This was the first hint she had been told of her new home.

Over time, the children came to trust and respect their new parents. They grew up, graduated from high school, and Sharon and Irene went on to marry and have children of their own. Bernice and Ron, now proud grandparents, still live on the farm, although Ron's nephew took over the management of the farm when Ron retired in 1994.

Would Bernice do it all again? She can't imagine what her life would have been like had she not met Ron. She had led a very quiet existence when she was single—dull and boring, in fact. When she asked Ron the same question ("Would you do it all over again?"), he simply answered, "Sure."

*Love, like joy, is meant to be our destiny.*
*It is here for all of us, and comes in unlimited abundance.*
*All we have to do is embrace it, in others and in ourselves.*

—Dinah Eng, journalist

# Kitty and L. D.

Kitty and L. D. married forty days after meeting through a newspaper ad. She was fifty years old; he was sixty.

Kitty was determined not to grow old alone. After moving to the Pacific Northwest from California to look after an ailing aunt, she placed an ad in the newspaper. L. D. says the ad caught his eye: "Honesty a must; dancing a plus!" He'd had a love of dancing since the age of five. Their first date lasted twelve hours as they danced the night away.

During her high school years, Kitty had not been allowed to date. This drastically dampened her social life and caused her to withdraw. Having low self-esteem and a severe case of acne didn't help matters either. "Who would want to date me?" she consistently asked herself. Another cause of stress was her older sister's immoral reputation. Kitty, who was righteous and moral, was embarrassed to tears by her sister's wanton behavior. Kitty feared being placed in the same category as her sister, so she kept to herself.

After graduation, Kitty attended college in Portland, Oregon, and lived with her favorite aunt. It was here that Kitty let her hair down and for the first time started to enjoy life. She befriended twin girls who lived next door and fell madly in love with their older brother, Ralph. Kitty and Ralph dated sporadically over the next few years, and even though Ralph was a big flirt, Kitty's loyalty was unwavering.

At age twenty-one, Kitty's life took a sudden turn for the worse: she was date-raped and lost her virginity. This left a permanent scar and changed her life forever. Fearing she might be pregnant, Kitty abruptly left Portland for San Francisco—she didn't want to bring shame upon her family, as they were still reeling from her sister's indiscretion of having a baby out of wedlock at age nineteen and giving her up for adoption—and she never let on why she was leaving town. As it turned out, Kitty was not pregnant, and soon afterward, she met Larry, a man who would significantly impact her life. She fell hopelessly in love. Six months into their relationship, however, Larry's company transferred him to another city. Soon their relationship dissolved, not because of the distance between them but because of some poor advice from a friend, who suggested she be more aggressive in her pursuit of Larry. Not wanting to lose him, Kitty followed that advice—and lost him anyway.

Broken-hearted and distraught, Kitty moved to a coastal town in Washington, which turned out to be dismal. She spent the greater part of the next two years there, until she could no longer stand it. She decided there were sunnier and more pleasant places to live, like Hawaii.

During Kitty's first year in Waikiki, Larry came to visit. At first, she could hardly contain her excitement and eagerly awaited his arrival, but she stood frozen to the spot when she saw him standing in the hotel lobby. All the pent-up, hurtful emotions she so carefully buried years before came rushing forth. She remembered all too well the pain of his rejection and abandonment. Gazing at him from afar, she realized that although she still loved him, she had disliked him for quite some time. She left him standing there.

Again, she moved on, requesting a transfer to California. From this point on, Kitty dated only casually. Her past experience proved, "Men don't hang around long if you refuse to have sex with them." No one interested her enough to want to hop into bed or get involved in a serious relationship, so for the next twenty-three years, she completely abstained. She kept herself busy working, sometimes two and three jobs at a time, and traveling.

At forty-eight years of age, Kitty returned to Portland, this time to nurse her ailing aunt, who was dying of cancer. She dearly loved her aunt and wanted her to be comfortable in her final years.

After Kitty's aunt died, the old familiar feelings of loneliness crept in. This time, she decided to take action. She placed an advertisement in the personal column in the local newspaper. L. D. responded. When they met, Kitty recalled L.D. was the nice man who had directed her to the personnel office when she stopped in at Sears looking for work a few weeks prior. Could this be fate?

*If you need something, and you can't get it in the conventional way,*

*if you leave yourself open to it, it will come in a way you never intended.*

—Gail Sheehy, author, journalist

## Connie and Peter

Connie and Peter met at work. They had both worked for the same company for twenty-five years. When they first met, Peter was married but lost his wife to cancer in 1987.

Connie was a real gadabout, traveling all over the world. When she returned from each trip, she entertained her coworkers by presenting a travel slide show at the office. Peter and his wife were ardent travelers, so they always looked forward to Connie's travel show. Connie's travel often was unorthodox—she would trek through third-world countries, sometimes in the back of a truck, pitch tents along the way, and eat porridge in the morning with crawly things in it.

In March 1993, both Connie and Peter were offered early retirement packages at work. At the time, Connie was fifty-eight and had not yet entertained the thought of retiring. When a financial counselor advised her to "take the money and run," she quickly decided to accept the package. When reality set in, she was so overcome with excitement, she dashed down to a friend's office, who kept a stash of 2-ounce liquor bottles confiscated from the airlines, cracked open a bottle of vodka, and downed it.

Shortly after she retired, Peter invited Connie and two other women from work to his apartment for dinner one evening. They all were good friends who had known each other over the past twenty-five years. The dinner conversation turned to ceiling fans—Connie noticed that Peter had one—and she mentioned that she wanted to buy a couple for her two bedrooms. Being the nice guy that he was, Peter offered to install them for her. Connie offered to cook dinner for him as a way to thank him. Before long, they were seeing each other exclusively.

Connie and Peter's love of travel led them to take many joint trips. They were compatible travelers and seemed to have a lot in common. On September 4, 1996, they stunned family and friends by sealing their love in a secret wedding ceremony in Bermuda. Peter was sixty-two; Connie was sixty-one.

This was Connie's first time at the altar. She had a real zest for life and previously had not given much thought to marriage—although several years earlier, a fortune teller had predicted that Connie would marry someone she had known for a long time whose name began with the initial P.

When she was in her early twenties, Connie was more interested in skiing and other sports activities than in men. She had dated a few men, but whenever the subject of marriage came up, Connie refused. She certainly never thought she would meet anyone through work; she had never been attracted romantically to her coworkers.

Connie does not regret waiting until age sixty-one to marry. Having babies was not high on her priority list. You could say she was a bit of a fatalist, believing if it was meant to be, it would happen.

Connie's friends questioned her wanting to get married at her age. Why not just live together? Connie preferred marriage over a live-in situation because she thought it was "more proper." Many have asked Connie how it feels to be married after being single for so long. Connie says, "I really don't feel married. I feel like I am living with an old friend. At our age, we don't try to impress each other. We accept each other as we are and haven't changed our characters at all. We are both down-to-earth."

*There is only one success . . .*
*to be able to spend your life in your own way.*

—Christopher Morley, American editor and author

# Lyndee and Elliott

At the time Lyndee met Elliott, she was thirty-nine; he was forty-one. They met at a tennis club, where they were both members.

One day prior to her tennis match, Lyndee dropped in at the gym to warm up. Someone else was on the StairMaster, so she used the time to stretch. During her stretching routine, she happened to notice a man (Elliott) looking at her. After her warmup, she was waiting in the foyer for her tennis partner to arrive when Elliott happened by. He introduced himself and struck up a conversation.

After that, Lyndee couldn't erase Elliott from her mind. He had it all going on: good looks, toned body, a nice personality—and the real plus: he was a tennis player. Coincidentally, Elliott had similar thoughts about Lyndee.

When Elliott called her the next day to join him for a drink, Lyndee eagerly accepted.

As their first date progressed, the idea that "this could be it" crept into her thoughts. They talked easily over a drink and continued their conversation on a stroll along the beach. Elliott bravely broached the subject of marriage and children. At first, she was startled, but when she realized this was his way of letting her know his intentions were serious, she silently congratulated him on his courage and breathed a sigh of relief that this topic was out of the way. By their second date, they were already sharing differences of opinion—it was election night.

Lyndee refused all dates except those with Elliott. It was a wildly exciting time, and she enjoyed every moment. It had been eons since she'd felt this strongly about any man. And the fact that he was a doctor also pleased her—it implied he had ability and intelligence. Intellectual stimulation always had been high on her priority list in her choice of men.

After two months of dating, Lyndee and Elliott moved in together. Three years later, they were married. They had a quiet wedding ceremony at their home and then flew to Provence, France, for a honeymoon.

Lyndee's love of travel was the primary reason she'd chosen a career as a flight attendant. She loved the excitement of visiting new places and meeting new people but claims her erratic schedule probably kept her from establishing a serious relationship and marrying at a younger age. Before she met

Elliott, however, the thought of marriage had never entered her mind.

Lyndee had three long-term relationships prior to her marriage. She was not one to waste time with a man if there was no attraction—there was no "let's wait and see."

Lyndee is glad she waited until after age forty to marry. She believes that with more maturity on their side, their marriage has a better chance of survival. If she had married sooner, she probably would have had children, but she now looks at this as a blessing in disguise. She loved her fun and her freedom, and when she finally did decide to marry, it was the right man and the right time.

*Never give up, for that is just the place and the time that the tide will turn.*

—Harriet Beecher Stowe, American author

## *Sue and Bert*

Sue and Bert met on a blind date. At first, she was bent on marrying someone at least ten years older than her, so when Bert came along, she didn't give him the time of day, even though he was a super-nice guy. In hindsight, Sue says, "The timing wasn't right for me."

She then rekindled a long-distance relationship with her first love and former fiancé, but it turned out to be the same old emotional roller coaster all over again. The same problems that had existed earlier resurfaced now—only magnified. The most positive thing that came out of trying a second time was that she was finally able to close the door and move on.

And then along came Bert . . . again. Sue was more receptive to accepting him into her life and allowing him to totally spoil her. All the things she had ever dreamed about in finding Mr. Right were now becoming a reality. She says, "I just needed to let go of a lot of baggage." She never thought she would find love again at age fifty-six, but she claims it's different than love at twenty-one. She appreciates the companionship more—someone to share the load, someone to travel with and laugh with.

Sue pinches herself sometimes, because she doesn't believe all the wonderful things that have happened to her since meeting Bert. She had been the giver in her relationships, whereas this time around, she is the recipient of lots and lots of love.

*If someone can take you to heaven, they can take you to hell.*

*Take back the power you gave them, and take yourself where you choose.*

—Alan Cohen, author

# *Sandy and David*

Sandy and David met on a blind date arranged by her sister. At the time, David was legally separated from his wife and waiting for their divorce to become final. Her sister originally had fixed him up with another friend who had children, but David wanted no part of that—his own four daughters were more than enough.

Sandy and David clicked on their first date. After dating for nine months, Sandy was curious whether she and David had a future together and decided she would give him an ultimatum, if this was not the case. She was ready to walk if he did not want to get married. They were married less than two years after first meeting. She was in her forties; he was fifty-two.

What had impressed Sandy the most about David was the fact that he was the one who wanted to keep his marriage together. She also loved the fact that his daughters were all in college, except one, who lived with David's ex-wife. (Four daughters could have been a huge obstacle, had they still lived at home.)

Sandy had dated a lot when she was single but had no long-term relationships. She was not optimistic that she would ever marry but nevertheless, she kept the dream alive in her heart, hoping the right man would come along. She thrived on being part of a couple, as did David. It raised her self-esteem, and she was finally able to let go of the Rodney Dangerfield kind of attitude—not wanting to join a club that would accept her as a member.

Luckily, Sandy did not want children. She envisioned all kinds of issues arising with a blended family. It was enough dealing with her mother-in-law, who played a key part in the dissolution of David's first marriage and caused friction in her and David's marriage. Sandy cautions singles to check out the whole package before getting involved—family, kids, in-laws, financial situation, and health. (A friend once commented, "When I meet a man, I'm not going to check out his bank account. I'm going to check with his doctor to make sure he's in good health.")

Sandy says the advantage of getting married later in life is that "you're more apt to tone down the wedding and spend your money on more practical things."

*Whatever the struggle, continue the climb.*
*It may be only one step to the summit.*

—Diane Westlake, author

## Linda and Sam

In the spring of 1999, when Linda was fifty-one, she received a call from Pam, one of her sister's best friends. "I'll bet you are wondering why I called," Pam said—and Linda did wonder; Pam previously had never called her.

Pam asked if Linda remembered Sam from high school; as it turned out, Linda did. He'd been a grade ahead of her. "Would you like to go out with him," Pam asked? Linda remembered Sam as a nice person, so she hesitantly agreed.

Sam was a veterinarian in a town about thirty-five miles south of Gainesville, Florida, where they had grown up and graduated from high school. One day, Pam took her dog to Sam, and they chatted about people they knew. Pam mentioned she had seen Linda recently, and Sam admitted he had always meant to ask her out in high school but had been too shy. Pam, trying to hide her exuberance, said, "It might not be too late."

Three weeks later, Pam arranged a cookout at her house, inviting Linda and Sam to attend.

When Linda had lived in Las Vegas, she had been in an on-again/off-again relationship. She tried to make it work but could not honestly tell him that she wanted to spend the rest of her life with him. She broke it off when she realized she was lonelier with him than without him. After having worked at various careers in Vegas—a singer, a blackjack dealer, and an interior designer—Linda decided to return to Gainesville, Florida.

She ended up working for a friend, whom she later dated, but just when they were starting to talk marriage, he was diagnosed with prostate cancer. Linda loved him deeply and was very thankful for the time they had together. He was very complimentary and told her wonderful things about herself that no one had ever told her before. It built her self-esteem, knowing that this wonderful man loved and cared about her. They spent eight wonderful years together before he died. After his death, she didn't have time to grieve; instead, she went on automatic pilot, tucking away her feelings and focusing on her obligations. Three years down the road, she started to have crying spells for no apparent reason. She thought she was losing her mind. As it turned out, she was finally grieving. She found a good clinical psychologist who helped her complete her grieving process in a constructive way. It was the best move she ever made. Later that year, her father died, and because of what she had learned, she was able to help other family members deal with their grief.

Linda had reached a point in her life when she was content to be alone. She had loved and had been loved. She took good care of herself, had fun, and enjoyed a large network of friends who sustained her. She walked a lot, often reciting a quote from the Bible: "Trust in the Lord with all your heart, lean not on your own understanding. In all your ways acknowledge him and he will direct your paths." She enjoyed her walks immensely; it was a time for her to be with herself and with God. At some point, she began paying attention to the goal-setting techniques she had learned. She began to write down the type of man she wanted to meet, and she didn't leave anything out—he had to love the water and be a good swimmer, be confident, be honest, be open, be present in the relationship without secrets or extramarital activities, and because she had no children, it was best that he didn't either. She also wanted someone she already knew. Sam was all that and more. As for the stuff she didn't include, Sam was that too.

Before the cookout, Linda received a call from Sam, saying he was looking forward to seeing her at Pam's. He called the next day, too, and then the day after that. They exchanged e-mail addresses, and this turned out to be a smart way to communicate, as it gave them an opportunity to get to know each other better. Linda always enjoyed getting to know someone through the written word, because the communication is without the benefit of facial expression, body language, voice inflexion, or emphasis on certain words. They both agreed it would be nice to get together prior to Pam's cookout, and so they met at a small café in Linda's neighborhood. They instantly recognized each other. Throughout dinner, Sam was a perfect gentleman, and after dinner, he said he wanted to meet her mother, with whom Linda was living at the time. Linda alerted her mother, and they drove the three blocks to her place. Sam and her mother liked each other instantly.

On the night of Pam's gathering, Linda arrived first and found a Vanda orchid from Sam waiting in the foyer for her. She found this intriguing. Both she and Sam enjoyed the evening and continued seeing each other on a regular basis. She wasn't quite sure if Sam was her type, but she was interested enough to get to know him better. He was sweet, kind, had a good sense of humor, and was very thoughtful. *What's not to like?* she asked herself.

Linda and Sam spent an adventurous summer together. One time, they rented a car to drive to St. Augustine so that Sam could purchase a collectible car. They planned to turn in the rented car and drive back in the new one, but the "new" car broke down, causing Sam to stress out. During the car episode, she remained calm, while he was at his wit's end. Linda determined that he was bothered by big things, whereas the little daily aggravations got to her. Amazingly, this brought them closer together.

A friend asked her once to describe Sam in one sentence. Linda responded with her first thought: "He has a pure heart. He is exactly the person he appears to be when you first meet him. He has no ulterior motives, no hidden agenda, and he is the finest man I've ever known."

In mid-August, on a lazy Sunday afternoon, Sam asked Linda to marry him. Without hesitation, her answer was yes.

Linda previously had been engaged five times—three times to the same man. She already had planned one wedding, and she had become accustomed to love turning sour. She didn't believe it would ever work out—until it actually happened. This time it was different. There was something different about Sam . . . and something different about her.

As it turned out, Sam was the answer to her prayers. They had a lot of similarities: family backgrounds, values, and they had been loved in the same way. Often, Sam mentioned he wished they had dated back in high school, but Linda reminded him,

"We are not the same people we were back then. We each had to grow into the people we have become."

Linda believes that their personal experiences were necessary in order to prepare them to meet each other. Sam was wounded in Vietnam and spent a year in rehabilitation. He had been married once before for twelve years. Linda truly believes that God has a plan for each of us, and it was obvious to her that the two of them were destined to be together. She believes Sam is the perfect man for her, and they met again at the perfect time.

Linda and Sam had a large wedding with lots of family and friends. It was the perfect beginning of their life together. Even though Linda once wondered if she would ever find him, she says, "Somehow, somewhere inside me, I knew there was someone for me."

*Live your spirit's dreams, not your mind's.*

—Alan Cohen, author

## *Leona and Cal*

Leona and her friend Mary were visiting in Palm Desert, California, and had to find accommodations for two extra days when their vacation was extended. On Valentine's Day, they were sitting in a hot tub at a tennis complex and struck up a conversation with a man named Fred. When they told Fred that all the hotels were booked because of the local Date Festival, and they needed a place to stay, Fred suggested they could stay at his friend Cal's place.

Leona and Mary agreed, and when Fred introduced them to Cal, he called them the "two virgins from Vancouver." Quick-witted Cal replied, "Do they have to leave that way?" Leona was instantly attracted to Cal's sense of humor. Cal turned out to be a gracious host and an extremely considerate man. To show their appreciation, when they returned home, Leona and Mary sent Cal thank-you gifts for his hospitality.

Over the next few months, Leona and Cal kept in touch. Cal was the first to extend an invitation to Leona, sending her a plane ticket to visit him and leaving it up to her to set the rules. Because of this flexible offer, she felt totally comfortable in accepting his generous invitation, and used her vacation time to visit him. The next year, when Leona lost her job, Cal gladly declared, "Pack your bags."

Leona spent the next four months in Southern California. When she first met Cal, he was adamant about never marrying again. Even so, she was a bit miffed when he told her, "I have nothing to offer you."

Cal's next visit to Vancouver found Leona acting somewhat aloof. Not until they openly discussed their last conversation in California, did Cal finally admit he did not want to let her go. This candid admission moved their relationship to a new level; they were now a couple.

When it came time for Leona to leave Cal in California the following year to secure another job in Vancouver, they talked about their feelings for each other. Neither of them wanted a long-distance relationship. Cal revealed, "I cannot imagine life without you." Leona quickly responded, "Are you proposing?" His answer was a strong yes!

Leona married Cal the following summer in Vancouver, three years after they'd first met. She was fifty-two years of age.

*What you run from, you run to.*

—source unknown

# Maggie and Fred

Maggie led a full and active life. She had the freedom to travel and did just about anything she wanted, when she wanted. She never felt compelled to get married. She was living in Los Angeles and had more single friends than married ones. But after living in L. A. for twenty-one years, Maggie moved back home after her father died—she didn't want to leave her mom on her own. "I'll only go for a short while," she promised herself.

At the urging of a girlfriend and her mother, Maggie tried online dating. At first, she was totally against it, but she finally acquiesced and decided to give it a try. Fred was one of the first men she dated. She liked him but didn't think he was her type, so she stopped seeing him after only a few dates. She went on to date several others.

Maggie would highly recommend online dating. She says it's good for one's ego. She claims it's a great way to meet suitable dating partners, especially as you get older—you meet men you wouldn't ordinarily meet. Even though the men she dated weren't all love matches, everyone she met was interesting and worth meeting.

Fred, as it turned out, was rather persistent and kept calling, even though Maggie didn't return his calls. Four months later, Maggie ran into Fred, which led to her finally agreeing to go out with him again. They were married less than one year later.

*People who love and believe in you do not need to be convinced, and people who do not love or believe in you are not worth trying to convince.*

—Alan Cohen, author

# Michelle and Jeff

(Story told in Michelle's words)

There are a few axioms I live by in my life, and they are part and parcel of my love story with my husband.

The first is "Good things come to those who wait," and the second is "When you least expect it, love will find you."

I did not marry until I was forty-five. I waited a long time, kissed a few frogs along the way, and when the time was right, Jeff came along. I met my husband in November 2000. We dated for six months, became engaged on April 13, 2001, and married on April 20, 2002.

A little about me . . . I come from an Italian American family; my mom was from Italy. I was raised in a strict household, where work always came before anything else, other than family. I didn't begin officially dating until I was seventeen (my senior year of high school). My dad talked my mom into letting me go out, as I would be off to college in a few months. My mother reluctantly agreed, and so began my dating adventures. They were limited, certainly, during high school, but in college, I began to discover myself as a young woman.

College, community service, and family occupied much of my time in my late teens and early twenties. I've had a career as an event coordinator since my mid-twenties, and I have worked hard getting to the point where I am now a professional.

Living on my own, I invested a great many hours in my job at Loyola Marymount University, and I dated occasionally. There were a few guys I was interested in, but looking back, I wasn't ready to settle down. I thrive on independence, and I was reluctant to get involved with someone who would tie me down.

With independence also came loneliness and the ever present desire to have kids—a family of my own. For a while, I looked for my prince, but it wasn't in the cards for me. At times I felt lonely—not pretty enough, not sexy or cute enough to attract anyone. I was actively involved in church work and in family life. I was conservative in my appearance and liberal in my politics. I wanted to positively affect our world through my work and community service.

Through these seeming contradictions, I trusted heavily in God and his will for me. He had blessed me abundantly throughout my life, and I had to believe he knew what he was doing. I just didn't appreciate fully his timeline for me! This went on for about fifteen years.

At the age of forty, I finally woke up. The decade started with news that I had to undergo major surgery, a hysterectomy. At first, I was devastated. I had always wanted to be a mommy, and my biological clock was winding down. Prayer and my supportive network reminded me that God would take care of me, and I believed good things would come of this difficult situation. I had been blessed in helping to raise my niece and nephew, which helped fill the void. My surgery was successful, and I felt so much better. During my recovery, I was determined to start moving as soon as I was able. In an odd way, I felt my spirit change a few weeks after surgery. I felt light and free. The eight-week rest from work was good for me.

I returned to work full time and immediately jumped back into a heavy load. As part of my work in Palm Springs, California, I worked with military bands from around the country and became good friends with some of the band staff at Marine Corps base Twentynine Palms. In 1999, the band staff adopted me as an "honorary Marine," and with that adoption was the expectation that I would work out regularly, doing physical training. (PT is an integral part of Marine Corps life.) I did it begrudgingly and with considerable whining, but I began to see my body change.

I learned to do pull-ups, and my arm and back muscles began to take great shape. I liked my appearance—a lot.

My dating life picked up. I was not looking for a serious relationship, but I found myself interested in someone with whom I used to work. It was a complicated situation, however, and our relationship did not work out. We remained friends, and looking back, I would not trade a minute of our time together, for it made me the person I am today.

November 10, 2000, was the day this fellow broke my heart. I was devastated but needed to turn my attention to work so that I could get through a planned event and not be distracted. Two days later, I had to attend a Veteran's Day parade. It was a cold, blustery winter day. I was tired from the last few days but had to put that aside to represent my employer at this parade. I was freezing as I stood outside, watching the parade. I noticed a gentleman standing near a bus that was designated for parade route transport. We started talking; he said his name was Jeff, and he invited me to sit and watch the parade from a warmer spot inside the bus. I readily accepted his invitation. He was tall, dark, and handsome, and we talked easily together. Jeff transported me to the post-parade reception, where we said good-bye. I silently kicked myself for not giving him my business card, but after the event, we ran into each other at

Walmart. Fate? Kismet? Who knows? I didn't forget to give him my business card this time, and so it began.

Jeff e-mailed me the following week and invited me to dinner. I thought, *Sure, why not?* I was still nursing my wounded heart and wasn't excited about dating, but I wanted an evening out. We met at a Thai restaurant, now one of our mainstays, and had a wonderful time talking and laughing. Jeff told me he was a retired marine and combat vet, having served in the first Gulf War. He shared some of his experiences as we continued to talk later into the evening, before saying a friendly good night.

We talked more during the following weeks; we dated, worked out, and got to know each other. We took it slowly and did not rush into anything hot and heavy. I began to think there was something special, something very different about this relationship. I wasn't running away, and neither was he. We readily accepted each other's situations at home: he was a widower raising two teenagers, and I was helping care for an ailing parent. We kept each other company, and we made each other laugh.

Six months after we met, we became engaged. I preferred a long engagement—fear began to creep in, but a long engagement also gave me time to plan the ideal wedding. We chose April 20, 2002, and decided to marry in San Diego, home of the Marine Corps Recruit Department. Jeff had been a drill instructor there, and I had spent time there attending an educators workshop. It is a special place for us and a refuge from Palm Springs.

Throughout the year of our engagement, we grew closer and closer. The relationship felt right for both of us. There were no doubts or hesitations, and I truly felt it was right, deep inside my bones.

Three weeks prior to the wedding, my mom suffered several strokes, the last one requiring life-extending decisions. It was a stress-filled time. My New York family flew out to see my mom. All this occurred during the final stages of the wedding planning. The week before the wedding was like a scene out of the movie *Moonstruck*, with the Italian family yelling and worrying; it was utter chaos.

The wedding went very well. It was a beautiful day, and everyone had a good time—although there was a huge twinge of sadness for me during the day, as my mom was dying and could not attend. I was having an amazing wave of emotions that whole week of the wedding. Jeff was the most supportive soul mate I ever could have chosen, and I give thanks to God for him.

We've gone through more challenges in the short time we have been married than many couples go through in a lifetime. We wouldn't have gotten through them without each other and a strong faith that has given us comfort and strength in the dark moments. There are more challenges ahead, no doubt, but we know that there also have been many blessings.

Currently, Jeff and I live between two homes. We live over seventy miles apart, and our time together is limited during the workweek. We made a conscious decision to have the kids finish high school where they had been living, rather than move them and cause additional trauma (they already had experienced trauma when they lost their mother). Good things come to those who wait, and finally, this year, we all will be living together in the same house. Amen!

A word about becoming a step mom: initially, the kids, Liz and Joe, had reservations when I came on the scene; they were still hurting over the loss of their mother. After Liz graduated from high school, the challenges with her began. She was discovering herself as a pretty young woman with a bit of a wild streak. She made difficult choices that affected the whole family, and we continue to learn about letting go and letting the kids learn for themselves. This is a hard job for parents, indeed.

When you marry when you're older, you realize time is short, and you must make the best of life in the years you have ahead. You learn to not sweat the small stuff, because there are too many important things that will be missed if you get caught up in minutiae. We've had to make adjustments—Jeff and I come from two very different worlds. He comes from a world of hard-earned service in the Marine Corps and is a quiet family man. I am a public figure and am fairly well recognized. Rarely do we go out somewhere that I do not run into someone who knows me. Jeff has had to adjust to this. While I am at public events, I am outgoing and assertive, whereas Jeff prefers to sit on the sidelines. I am learning to be more sensitive to his position and respect his desire to take a backseat, while I work the crowd at a concert or an event.

I was used to taking care of myself—making my own decisions, doing my own work, handling my own financial and professional affairs, doing my own laundry, and cooking my own meals. Some of this has changed for the better: Jeff and I both do laundry; we cook together and are joining forces on the financial issues. Letting go isn't as hard as one might expect. We each have our own strengths and weaknesses and are merging the best of both sides. Most important, I find myself not wanting to be so independent. I want my husband to help take care of me, to be by my side—from cooking together in the kitchen to sitting with me at the hospital when Dad is ill. I need Jeff. He completes me, and I wouldn't want it any other way.

The world has changed radically since September 11, and so have my personal thoughts and beliefs when it comes to our freedom and being attacked by terrorists. My sentiments and political tendencies have changed tremendously from my early years in community service. I look at the world differently now that I'm married to a marine (retired or not) and have a stepson entering the Marine Corps. As a wife and mother, and as an "adopted marine" myself, my heart jumps each time I hear of deployments of dear friends or news of reactivating retirees. I fully support my husband and my stepson and their choices, and I would give my life in support of their right to defend our country. I admire their willingness to put it on the line for all of us, if needed. I am offended by folks who don't value the price that others have paid for our freedom in this country, which for me is a 180-degree turn from my earlier politics. Amazing what love does to you and for you.

I have been abundantly blessed with Jeff in my life, and I can only believe God will continue to bless us both abundantly with each other.

*The answer will come. Direction will come. You will know.*

—Alan Cohen, author

# Darlena and Bob

(Written in Darlena's words)

In 1988, while I was working at a mental health center, a psychic was brought in to teach us how to communicate with people who were unable to communicate well. She taught us how to read people physically. She chose me for her demonstration. Before she started, she looked me in the eye and said, "Do you know that there is a guy in the Bay area who is looking for you? He got divorced about a year ago and has custody of his two kids. He's half Irish and half Scottish." Everyone looked dumbfounded. Why was she telling us this? She continued, saying that he was working in an office nearby, and although she couldn't quite read his last name, it began with either Mc or Mac. Everyone was abuzz except for me. I really did not think much about it for nearly ten years.

In early 1998, I was dating a man at work who was very dashing, but I knew he was a fling. When I found out he was married, I immediately broke it off with him. I was not as devastated as I would normally have been; in fact, I felt liberated. I decided against having another boyfriend; it was too much of a hassle.

A few days later, our corporate banker came into our office to say the bank was running a contest, and the winners would go to the Carmel Valley Ranch Hotel to play golf in the Silicon Valley Golf Tournament. He asked if he could enter my name. I agreed, never thinking I would win. A few weeks later, it was announced that I was one of the winners.

I was then contacted and asked what my handicap was. I said, "*What* handicap?" I hadn't realized I'd have to enter the golf tournament. Fortunately, the winners could invite another person, so I ran around the office trying to find someone to play in the golf tournament with me. After a few days of unsuccessful looking, I asked my office mate what I should do. She suggested I search for a golfer on AOL. I just typed in what I was looking for: "Anyone willing to golf in a tournament in Carmel . . ."

Before long, I received a reply from a man named Bob McChesney, a divorced father who had custody of his two kids. He was skeptical of my offer. "What are you up to?" he asked. "Are you selling something?" Once I told him the whole story, he agreed to go. We talked on the phone a few times and he sent his golf scores and stats to the people running the tournament. He was accepted.

True to the psychic's prediction, our amazing love story began. We are now happily married and living the life we were meant to live together.

*The world you see is a stage you have constructed with your thoughts, and everyone you meet is an actor you have hired to play out the script you have written.*

—Alan Cohen, author

## $\mathcal{J}$udi and $\mathcal{S}$am

At age sixty, Judi wanted to get married. She had been alone for a long time and was ready to connect with the right man.

A woman Judi worked with had been discussing a breakup with her boyfriend, Sam. At the time, Judi did not pay much attention, but some time later, her ears perked up when friends wanted to introduce her to a man also named Sam—the same Sam who had broken up with her coworker.

On Judi and Sam's first date, he asked her where she worked. Right up front, Judi told him where she worked—the same performing arts theater where his former girlfriend worked—and she added, "Yes, I do know your ex." She was relieved to learn that was not an issue for him. They set another date the following week.

The next week, Judi's phone rang at precisely the date and time Sam said he would call. From that point on, their relationship took off.

Sam lived up to Judi's top three priorities for husband material: he was brilliant, he was funny, and he asked questions and was a good listener.

While they were getting acquainted, Judi's boss announced his wedding plans and invited everyone to the ceremony. Judi hadn't told her coworker that she was dating Sam, but now she knew she had to come clean with her. At the boss's wedding, Sam and her pal greeted each other cordially in passing, and all was well.

Soon afterward, Judi and Sam announced their engagement. Because they had been spending so much time at Sam's, he suggested that Judi move in with him. Judi was adamant, saying, "I'm not moving in; I'm getting married." Sam agreed, and they immediately immersed themselves in wedding plans. Judi had a blast planning their wedding, and Sam had just as much fun watching her.

Judi and Sam's beautiful wedding took place at an upscale restaurant in Palm Desert, California, with 150 people in attendance; a hundred more than Judi had planned, but Sam wanted to invite a lot of his friends.

House renovations began, as soon as the happy couple settled in together. They were in sync as far as esthetics were concerned, so the decisions were easy. At the same time, Judi's life at the office began to pick up speed. As manager of special events, she was putting together her first big gala. The stress of it all caused back problems for her, but it was a treat to have Sam at home, ready to provide the tender loving care she needed and to cook dinner—truly a man with a good heart.

Everyone had assumed Judi would never get married. They thought she would have difficulty making concessions after having been single for so many years. Not so! She not only found it invigorating to have someone with her, but she wondered why everyone was concerned. "It's nice to have someone who has your back." She never felt like she was compromising; instead, she saw it as an education, opening up her life to something new. Sam introduced her to opera; and she introduced Sam to country music. Sam's daughters were another positive point in the marriage. It was mutual love and admiration between her and his two daughters, and she found it immensely gratifying to experience being a grandmother to his four grandchildren.

One of the main reasons Judi had not rushed into marriage during her younger years was because she was in constant motion. She traveled a lot while building her career. She enjoyed life to the fullest and thought nothing could entice her to give it up—until she met someone who made her life richer. Sam was that man. "Sometimes you don't even know what you are looking for until you stumble upon it," Judi mused.

Judi's advice to anyone looking for love is to make yourself visible—get out and about and open yourself up to meeting new people, going to new places, taking classes, joining groups, going to wine tastings, or attending parties. And tell everyone you know that you are available. It's a numbers game.

*Great adventures await those who are willing to turn the corner.*

Chinese saying

## *Sherrill and Don*

Sherrill and Don met when they both worked at a county health department. She was supervisor of the budget unit, and he was in the revenue management section. Every time she requested revenue figures from him to complete her monthly report, he would say, "Come and get them." This annoyed Sherrill immensely, and she couldn't help labeling Don obnoxious.

Later on, Sherrill's friend Alice went to work for Don. Alice and Don often went to lunch together and frequently asked Sherrill to join them, which she did. One day, Alice was sick, so Sherrill joined Don for lunch on her own. Over lunch, they discussed Alice's recent breakup with her boyfriend, and when Don genuinely showed concern, Sherrill saw him in a more favorable light and started to warm up to him. Slowly, a friendship developed between them.

Because neither was dating anyone, Don suggested he and Sherrill get together for a movie one night. Sherrill declined, not wanting to get involved with anyone. When she mentioned it to Alice, Alice suggested that Sherrill accept Don's offer of a movie—but be honest, telling Don it was "friends only." Don readily agreed to those terms and then added, "If I was going to ask anyone out on a date, it would be someone much younger—a potential marriage partner." Sherrill was taken by surprise by his blatant remark but somewhat impressed by his honesty. She later learned this was all a facade; he was a schemer and had designed a specific plan to win her over. They dated exclusively over the next two months, but Don kept their relationship strictly platonic—also part of his plan.

One day they took a day trip up to Santa Barbara, stopping off at a roadside wine shop to have a bite to eat and taste the wine. It seemed so natural for Sherrill to lean over and give Don a kiss. She was becoming fond of him and wanted to express it. Don, on the other hand, maintained his guard, keeping their relationship platonic. When he dropped her off that night, he gave her a quick kiss good night and drove off. He continued to follow his strategic plan, even to the extent of persuading his boss to hire Sherrill.

It took another ten months before Don brought up the subject of marriage. He casually broached the subject, saying, "I was thinking . . . we should get married." Sherrill, equally as nonchalant, said, "You know . . . you are right." It may not have been the most romantic proposal, but it was comfortable for both of them, and it felt right.

They got married at the Hotel Bel-Air in Los Angeles in a beautiful garden setting—this had been Sherrill's childhood dream. When she visited the hotel for the very first time with her parents as a young girl, she declared, "This is where I want to get married."

Sherrill had had a couple other serious relationships in her life—one during college, one after—but the timing had been all wrong for her. At the time she met Don, Sherrill had intentionally stopped dating because she was not impressed with the dating scene. She was quite content with her life. She had purchased her first house and had bought a refrigerator and a stove. It pleased her immensely that she was able to make these purchases without seeking advice from anyone. She became a woman of independence. Even so, with Don, it just seemed right.

Now happily married and both retired, Sherrill and Don spend their winters in the California desert and their summers in Washington State. Not a day goes by when Don doesn't tell Sherrill how much he loves her. She says, "Even when I'm mad and not talking to him, he becomes a nuzzler and won't let up until I return his affection, which is a good thing."

Sherrill's advice to women who are still looking for that special man to share their lives: "Pursue your own dreams, and be comfortable with who you are." She was not open to Don until she had reached this point in her life.

Don's perseverance and wanting to go slow so he wouldn't scare her off persuaded Sherrill to change her mind about him. Fate sometimes has a way of intervening and altering our destinies.

*The more you praise and celebrate your life,
the more there is in life to celebrate.*

—Oprah Winfrey

# PART II

*Getting Back In The Game*

## Chapter 1

# Why Isn't a Nice Girl Like You Married?

This is a difficult question to answer, especially when you've run out of clever responses. You definitely want to come up with something unique, rather than the same old lame excuse of not having met the right one. Here are a few that might give them pause:

- If I tell you, I'm going to have to kill you.
- I don't want to be another divorce statistic.
- Fifty percent of marriages fail. Why would I want to be one of them?

- I am afflicted with the grass-is-always-greener syndrome.
- I like my own space, and I don't want to share it.
- I'm busy right now.

Most single women have had the opportunity to get married, but obviously, something or someone stood in their way.

Fortunately, being single does not have the same stigma as it had in the past—at least we're not referred to as spinsters anymore, except on a marriage license. In Anita Shreve's book, *A Wedding in December,* she describes what her character, Agnes, thought of the word spinster: "A hateful word even to say in her thoughts, not only because of its antiquated and insulting nature but also because it suggested a bloodless woman of indeterminate age." Look at the television show *Sex and the City*. It shows you can be single and be sexy, you can live the life you want, and you can have strong connections with your girlfriends, who are always there to support you over the rough spots.

Not all women are desperate to find a man. Some would rather focus their energy on their careers, their children, or traveling. I'm sure, however, that most women would like to be dating men who are exciting, attractive, and interesting; someone who finds them exciting, attractive and interesting. Unless we are extremely lucky in love, we often have to kiss a lot of toads before we meet the handsome prince.

It's not that most single women can't get married; it's usually because they have not found that special person who turns the pilot light back on, ignites the flame, and turns up the heat—the one who makes them feel special. Timing is everything. The funny thing is, it usually becomes the right time when we have changed our focus and it's no longer an issue, or sometimes when we've given up altogether. Life has a way of changing all this once we let go of having to have a relationship.

Some time ago, I was watching comedian Tracy Smith on a *Comedy Central* television show. She was talking about what her dating life was like when she was younger. She said, "I used to go through men like a box of Kleenex. Then I turned thirty . . . and I started digging through the trash can, trying to find the wad I had thrown away. Where's that guy that liked me too much? Where's the guy that was too nice? What was I thinking?" Can you relate? I certainly can.

There are reasons why some women stay single longer. There are fears, hurts from past relationships that are not so easy to let go, difficulty working through the father/daughter issues from childhood, holding on to feelings of love for someone who has moved on, and hundreds of other reasons. We are the only ones who can choose to open ourselves up to new learning and unlock those fears so that we can move forward.

Through much reading, I've learned that whatever is happening in our lives is coming from the image we hold about ourselves. This image we project out into the world attracts like situations into our lives. So, if we have a poor self image we will not attract the kind of man we truly desire, instead, we'll attract a man we believe we deserve. A way to change this outcome is by first changing the vision we have of ourselves. When we learn to love and accept ourselves we will start to attract the kind of man who sees our better qualities and who is more in line with our true selves. A close friend once asked me, "What changed within yourself prior to your meeting your husband?" Off the top of my head, I responded, "I was completely comfortable in my own skin." If I could relate it to tennis, I would say, it was like being on the top of my game.

Some women immediately drop their friends as soon as there is a new man in their lives. This is a sure way to lose a guy in 10 days. If you cut yourself off from your friends and the activities you previously enjoyed, you lose a part of who you were and, perhaps, why he found you attractive in the first place. The relationship with you has to work first; otherwise, it puts too much pressure on the relationship having to work out. It should be your top priority.

Steps to building your most important asset—self-esteem:

- Nourish yourself mentally, physically, and spiritually. ✓
- Do more things you truly enjoy each day—eliminate the "shoulds."
- Exercise—it builds your shape along with your self-esteem.
- Expand your circle of friends, those who bring out the best in you.
- Ignite your passion; be inspired by new learning.
- Donate your time to a worthy cause; be of service to others.
- Simplify—Get rid of anything and everything you don't use or want.
- Create a new you with a makeover—update wardrobe, cosmetics, hairdo.
- Maintain an attitude of gratitude; your blessings will continue to expand.
- Be irresistible; let go of neediness.
- Be interesting; be interested.
- Be spontaneous; live in the moment.
- Each year, explore new places and try new things.

## Chapter 2

# Turning Point: Letting Go and Moving On

I think we all have a turning point—a time in our lives when an event or circumstance causes us to pause, possibly freak out, and then to make a radical shift in our perspective and to move on in a more positive direction.

My turning point came at age forty-two. I got involved in a relationship with a close friend's ex-love, with whom she still got together with occasionally. Normally, I avoided such entanglements like the plague, but I was drawn into this scenario with magnetic force, lacking the personal power to resist his charm and undivided attention. In my defense, I was unemployed for the first time in my life—by choice, but I couldn't have guessed such overwhelming feelings of vulnerability and insecurity would surface, causing me to let my guard down and get involved in such a precarious situation. It also blinded me to his deviousness in playing us both. Finally, I did come to my senses and blurted out the truth to my friend. It did not surprise me when she chose to hang on to his friendship rather than mine. What followed was the devastating impact of losing both relationships and dealing with (at least what seemed at the time) insurmountable disappointment in myself. I was not proud of the way I handled the situation. I was acting completely out of character.

Even though this experience was traumatic, and I suffered the loss of a good friend, it was life-changing, for which I am grateful. It caused me to spend the greater part of the next decade in deep reflection, questioning my involvement in such a predicament and not honoring my values. I removed myself from the dating scene altogether, except for a few casual friendships, and spent my time with good friends, traveling, taking courses, and being actively involved in sports. Today, I look back on this incident and firmly believe that if it hadn't happened the way it did, in such a tumultuous fashion, I would not have sought out a good counselor who pressed all the emotional buttons (buried treasure) and helped me come to an understanding and forgive myself – and to move on.

## Chapter 3

## Commitment Phobia

During my youth, my idea of commitment was so confining that I'd retreat every time a relationship took on serious overtones. A challenge kept my interest alive; professions of love caused me to take flight and look elsewhere, and I was afflicted with the grass-is-always-greener syndrome.

During a Context Training Corporation self development training program, founded by Randy Revell, popular back in the mid-80's, I learned there are no greener pastures. A change in circumstance does not change your experience. A shift in context, a different way of viewing your circumstance, determines your experience. Many people think by changing partners they will be happier. And, sometimes they will, but only if they change or look closely at the real reason they left their previous relationship. Unless you deal with the problem it doesn't go away, it's called baggage. It's like Velcro, it sticks with you.

Lack of commitment means sitting on the fence, unable to make a decision, and allowing fears to hold us back. Two things can happen when one person within a relationship decides to commit: either the other person also has strong feelings and the courage to commit, or decides he/she does not feel the same way and is not ready to commit to the relationship.

At a Context Training five-day workshop, we were asked to determine our focus prior to attending—the obstacle we wanted to confront and overcome. Mine was commitment—or so I thought. By the end of the workshop, I was keenly aware that it was not commitment I feared most; it was rejection and abandonment. (I'm not sure where this came from; it could have stemmed from losing my parents at a young age, along with the secure feeling of being loved unconditionally.) Until we know what our demons are, it is difficult, if not impossible, to confront them and to move past them. I was able to redefine "commitment" in a more acceptable and positive light. As David and I got deeper into our relationship, at no time was I inclined to back away. My past commitment fears never surfaced. I believe he was the catalyst to my overcoming commitment phobia.

## Chapter 4

## Endings—or Is It Beginnings?

When a friend's relationship ended, and she was going through withdrawal pains, we communicated with a flurry of e-mails back and forth. What came out of this frantic e-mailing was a new perspective.

We only feel pain when a relationship ends if we feel the man leaving not only takes his love away, but takes away the love we feel for ourselves with him, leaving us feeling rejected and abandoned. However, if our self-esteem is at an all-time high, we are less likely to be affected to such an extent. We will find it easier to let go and move on knowing that there is a good possibility we will meet someone else who is able to return our love. By keeping ourselves engaged in activities we enjoy, and with the support of genuine friends who have our best interests at heart, we are less likely to unravel when a relationship falls apart. Feeling good about who we are and having a positive outlook is a huge magnet for attracting the next person into our lives. This person will be unable to resist the person we are becoming.

Jan Denise, author of *Naked Relationships*, and author of Inside Relationships Newspaper Column says: "Endings are really transitions" . . .

"A breakup is not merely an ending. It is a transition, a path to a new beginning. And you get to embark on it with more wisdom. . . . If we received a report card at the end of each relationship, it would take some of the guesswork out of transition. We would know where we stood—which classes we passed and which ones we needed to work harder in. If you did not expend much effort, that may be a major source of your pain. You may be beating yourself up with could-haves and should-haves. Stop. Evaluate your own progress. Use your regret to learn the lesson rather than demoralize yourself. Look at what you could have done as well as what you will do next time—and do it with your existing partner if you can. It's never too late to improve your grade. Look at how your relationship has played out. Look at what it was designed to teach you. Learn it and use it to your advantage. And you will one lesson at a time, move on to live more of the dream. *"*

Iyanla Vanzant, author of *In the Meantime: Finding Yourself and the Love You Want*, says, "You cannot lose anything that has been divinely ordained for you. It will come back when you are ready to receive it. If you let go of something or someone that has not been divinely ordained for you, you are making room for something else to come into your life. There is never a good reason to fear that you are wrong or that you are losing. Fear only delays fulfillment."

When asked why the road curves, Vanzant's friend Joie says, "You would not have been able to handle it before now. That's why the road curves. It provides us with the opportunity to take in a little at a time. As we move forward, covering more ground, a little more is revealed to us. That's how life works. It gives you what you can handle in small doses, even when you think you are able to handle more. It is called the grace of God."

To love is to risk. The alternative is loneliness. The only way we grow is through our relationships with others—they reflect back to us who we are. It's like looking in the mirror.

107

Whatever we feel that marriage or having a man in our lives will give us—confidence, emotional or financial security, love, companionship, humor, or whatever—it is the quality we need to develop within ourselves in order to magnetize someone with these qualities into our lives. As Sanaya Roman states in her book, *Living with Joy*, "To feel secure, you need to feel you are growing, expanding, and enlarging the scope of your world."

Think of a relationship as a safe place where we can comfortably and freely express ourselves; where we can ask for and receive emotional support when we need it and get a gentle push when we are not aware it is essential at the time. A relationship is not something we desperately need to fill a void. I like to think of it as giving me a soft place to land.

If you strongly desire to have a man in your life, you'll do whatever is necessary to make it happen. Once you commit, the "how" will magically appear. Remember: "When one definitely commits oneself, then providence moves, too."

***Let your intuition be your guiding light.***

## Chapter 5

# Risking

After reading David Viscott's book *Risking*, I learned that the real strength in a relationship comes from having the confidence to express our needs and by allowing ourselves to be vulnerable. The level of security we feel within ourselves dictates how comfortable we are in expressing our feelings and letting others see our authentic selves. It is a risk worth taking, because through the freedom of expressing our feelings, we create the space for the other person to open up and respond in kind. If we choose not to honor our feelings and ignore them thinking they are not important, or they will not be well received, we are doing ourselves a disservice. This could prevent the relationship from reaching a deeper and more enriching level.

One of the most important risks in a relationship is being candidly honest when we express our feelings. Fear of exposing ourselves and being vulnerable forces us to hold back a little. By not allowing this freedom of expression prevents the other person from getting to know us on a deeper level. No relationship is worth having if we need to constantly guard our true feelings and pretend they do not exist. Eventually, the relationship will start to break down because it will be impossible to keep up this façade.

**Moving Forward**

Japanese Morita and Naikan, claim the best way to move forward rather than let the unknown hold us back, is to do it anyway. They believe that any positive action, no matter how minor, feeds our self-worth. By taking a step forward, it will build the strength of character to act, despite our fears. For example, if we are afraid to change careers, we should accept our feelings of anxiety, but proceed forward by updating our resume and setting up interviews anyway. Taking a risk and stepping carefully into the unfamiliar is the only way we will discover what the future holds for us. This wisdom can also be applied to a relationship.

*Chapter 6*

# The Dating Game

"When will waiting for the one be done?"

—*Sex and the City television show*

If you treat dating as a game, you most likely will enjoy the process. Otherwise, it can be an anxiety-ridden, nail-biting, stomach-churning, confidence-busting, heart-pounding, distasteful experience. You don't want to go there. On the other hand, it can be an exhilarating, memorable, exciting, life-changing experience.

Anywhere you are and in any situation, you can change the ordinary into the extraordinary by paying attention to who is sitting or standing next to you and by striking up a conversation.

*Listen Up!* The stigma of the older woman-younger man scenario is non-existent in the current dating arena. Many older women, affectionately known as "cougars", openly date younger men. If she has looked after herself, stayed healthy and fit, she is more apt to attract and be attracted to a younger man, whereas a younger man will seek an older woman because of her appeal, the idea of more experience, and her affluence. She is more in touch with who she is, knows what she wants and with whom she would rather spend time. She has carved out a comfortable lifestyle for herself filled with activities she enjoys, surrounded by good friends, and she has adapted to living on her own. She would not readily disrupt her status quo in order to create space for him in her life, unless she felt he was well worth the gamble.

At the beginning, don't take yourself too seriously, and don't take your date too seriously. After a few dates you will know if he's a 'date of interest' and whether he has your best interests in mind. *Don't read more into what he says than what he actually says.* Too many women hang on to every word a man tells them, or if he doesn't say what they want to hear, they interpret it in the best possible light—in other words, they make excuses for him. Be realistic! There is no urgency in the dating process—let the relationship evolve at its own speed.

A must read for all singles is *He's Just Not That Into You* by Greg Behrendt and Liz Tuccillo. It's the no-excuses truth to understanding guys. This book reveals how easily we let men off the hook and believe what they tell us, especially if we want the relationship to work. All the signs are there, but it's like we have blinders on. We'd rather make excuses for their broken promises, forgotten calls, and no-shows, when all they want sometimes is a warm body. Behrendt openly admits he's used all the lame excuses. As Tuccillo says in her account, she would rather "believe that men are too scared, too stressed, too sad, too spiritual, too angry, too fat, too crazy, too in love with his ex-girlfriend, too sensitive, too sunburned, too in love with his mother, too homicidal, too anything, than find out that he's really just not attracted to me."

Behrendt believes, "we all deserve better, and that if women truly believe it and are open to it, they will find a good person to love."

Dating is a process. On each date, we let our guard slip a little, revealing more of our personality. Get into the moment—go beyond small talk. Be interested in him and what he's all about. Hopefully, he'll respond in kind. If he doesn't, be aware he may be too self-absorbed, and your feelings will always take second place to what's going on within him.

Suggest interesting and fun things to do together that are conducive to talking—without a lot of alcohol. You don't want to be too loose-lipped and reveal too much too soon. Leave some of the mystique, which is the magnet that keeps drawing him back to learn more about you.

As your relationship evolves, you'll discover whether you share the same values, whether you enjoy the same activities, whether you have the same sense of humor (this is important; you could both be laughing at your own jokes rather than each others), and whether you are physically and romantically in sync. It all has to work. Listen to what your heart is telling you.

If he does not call when he says he will, move on, but don't take it personally. It is not you; it's him. And later on when you do meet the man who makes your heart sing, you will be only too pleased that the other guy didn't call.

## Pursuing our Passion

To keep our energy and attractiveness at a high level, we need to continue to pursue our interests and our passions by staying involved in activities we enjoy and by opening ourselves up to making new friends. Forget the ones with the negative attitudes; they'll only drag you down. I'll never forget a woman I met at a party. She was a lot younger than I, but she held me spellbound with her talk of travel, meeting interesting people, and trying new jobs. She was definitely open to new challenges. On a whim, she quit her job and traveled to Greece to start anew. She ended up working in a restaurant for a while, something she had never done before. Initially, she was terrified, but soon her fears turned into excitement. She met new friends and gradually started adapting to her new environment. Think of what she can tell her grandchildren about her life—it will be much more intriguing than complaining about her latest aches and pains.

Years ago while attending a retreat, we were asked to picture ourselves at an old age, and then retrace our steps back from that age to our present age, filling in the blanks. We were asked to describe what events, exciting times, interesting people, new learning, and challenges we wanted to relive at a ripe old age. This exercise was quite revealing. I had envisioned myself writing and painting, not something I had given a thought to back then, but is presently inching its way into my life. James Dean, the actor who was killed in a car accident at a young age, once said, "Dream your dreams as if you'll live forever, but live your life as if you'll die tomorrow."

It's important to keep our lives exciting—doing what we love to do, in the company of those we love. Whatever lights up our lives and brings us joy is what we need to incorporate more of into each day. It will not only bring out the best in us, but will make us more interesting and loving human beings.

A man enjoys being around a woman who is having fun and being herself and who is not desperately seeking a man. And he especially likes a woman who is interested in finding out more about him.

## TODAY'S MEETING PLACES

Meeting places have changed, although we can still meet men in the same places as we always have—at parties, dances, bars, and on blind dates. Also, don't rule out meeting men at work, through friends, while taking a course, or while playing a sport or attending your favorite sporting event. And don't forget about traveling—you never know who you will meet at your destination, or along the way.

> *Often we meet an interesting man when we least expect it*
> *—usually when our focus is on something else.*

In today's world, however, a lot of older women are connecting with men on the various dating sites through the Internet, believing their chances of connecting with someone their own age and who shares similar interests are far greater.

Online dating has made it more convenient for singles to search for love comfortably situated in their own homes, rather than hanging out in bars. www.Match.com; www.eHarmony; www.plentyoffish.com (POF is a free site) are just a few of the numerous Internet dating sites.

The secret of dating is to maintain a good attitude, put on a happy face, believe in miracles, and stay open to conversing with the opposite sex whenever an opportunity presents itself. If you think someone is interesting, make an effort to connect. We are naturally drawn to people with great smiles, good attitudes, who are approachable and easy going, and who have a good sense of humor—which is number one on most lists—men and women.

**Placing an Advertisement**: About twenty years ago, seven of my friends and I decided to place an advertisement in the newspaper for eight men to make up a dinner party of sixteen. We had a blast! The most fun was receiving the letters and photos and then deciding who to invite. It stands out as a memorable experience. We held the dinner at a friend's high-rise apartment in the West End of Vancouver. It started out with a comical incident. We were unaware the men all had arrived, arms laden with flowers and wine but unable to announce themselves on the intercom, because it was not working. They must have wondered if the invitation was some kind of sick joke. My girlfriends and I, however, could not figure out why everyone was late. We finally figured it out, and someone went downstairs to collect them. As the men walked in, it was difficult not to break out in fits of laughter, because it felt like we were in a receiving line at a wedding. Although no hot romances resulted from our dinner party, a great time was had by all, and there were a few calls back and forth afterward. If you want to replicate such a fun time today, a good place for an advertisement would be in the business section of the newspaper, where most men would be sure to see it.

**Getting Acquainted Dinner Parties**: Each woman invites a male friend to introduce to her single girlfriends. Friends of mine had hosted such parties. My friend, Kathy, met her boyfriend, David, by inviting him to one of these parties. It was through the suggestion of a mutual friend, who suggested she invite, David, who had recently broke up with his girlfriend. Kathy followed his suggestion and invited him to one of these parties. As it turned out, he was going to be out of town. However, when he returned, he called asking her out on a date. Twenty years later, they are still together.

A creative friend of mine once held a party she titled "New Pick'ns for Spring Chick'ns." She'd met a few nice men while on a ski vacation and once she returned home, she decided to throw a party, inviting them as well as some of her other single friends. She wanted to kick-start her love life, which had been dormant longer than she wanted to admit. It was at this party that she met her husband—he was one of the skiers.

## A Flash from the Past

Have you ever thought of getting in touch with a boyfriend from your past, perhaps a high school sweetheart or a college romance? There are websites that reunite school chums. A good book that may encourage you to do this is *My Boyfriend's Back* by Donna Hanover. This book includes true stories of rediscovering love with a long-lost sweetheart, as well as offering great advice on how to connect and why this love is so irresistible.

## Tips for Dating over Fifty

(Maggie Downs' column, *The Desert Sun* newspaper, Palm Springs, California)

- *Remember that there are many single people your age looking for someone, and they feel exactly the way you do.*
- *The people you meet will have a past. Expect them to accept yours and be open enough to accept theirs.*
- *Dress in ways that make you feel good about yourself.*
- *Go to places where you feel comfortable.*
- *Slow down; don't rush. That date isn't the last one available.*
- *Use the Internet to find age-appropriate people.*

## Tips for Dating at Any Age

(Maggie Downs' column, *The Desert Sun* newspaper, Palm Springs, California)

- *Flirt at least once a day. It's practice. Flirt with the pool man, the person in the car next to you at a stop light. Flirting can be as simple as smiling and making eye contact and holding it five or ten seconds longer than normal.*

- *Go out at least once a week to social situations where you can meet potential mates—cocktail parties, singles events, golf tournaments, art gallery openings, happy hour at a local bar, lectures at your local church, etc. Go by yourself. Dress to impress. Be open and receptive so that others might approach you.*

- *Go out with everyone who asks you. It's practice. You want to practice on people you're not interested in, so that when someone special comes along, your dating skills will be honed.*

- *Go out with someone three times before making a decision about him. Give him a chance. Don't rule him out too quickly; you might grow to love him.*

- *A person is either attracted to you or he isn't. Don't try to impress someone who clearly isn't interested in you.*

- *Men want sex and are willing to trade intimacy to get it; women want intimacy and are willing to trade sex to get it. This doesn't change after age fifty—it's still pretty much the norm at any age.*

- *There is a perception among women over fifty that there are no good men available. If you believe that's true, it is. If you don't believe it's true, then it's not. It's all in your attitude and expectations. You see what you believe.*

## Additional tips from other women:

Say "Hasta La Vista, Baby" if he . . .

- ➤ constantly talks about himself
- ➤ refers to his last girlfriend on a regular basis
- ➤ stands you up just once, without calling
- ➤ ogles other women when he is with you
- ➤ doesn't ask you any questions about yourself or your life
- ➤ doesn't take you out of his apartment or yours
- ➤ leaves his wallet on the piano too many times
- ➤ is unpopular with your friends
- ➤ doesn't have many friends of his own, and you don't like the ones he does have
- ➤ seems to have a mysterious past

## Understanding the Opposite Sex

One of the best books I've read on this subject is *Men Are from Mars, Women Are from Venus* by John Gray, Ph.D—an oldie but goodie. It was especially important to learn that when men "go into their caves" (get quiet to sort out their thoughts), it is mandatory not to give any advice or try to fix them or to bring them out. They need to be left alone until they are ready to reconnect with us. For years, I thought it was because they were bored and ready to move on. If a man does not have an opportunity to pull away, he never gets a chance to feel a strong desire to reconnect and be close to us again. So leave him alone until he is ready to come out of his cave. (Don't leave him alone too long, though, or he might find someone else in that cave.)

John Gray stated: "The feelings that come up whenever you feel someone is rejecting you—or when you don't feel special anymore—are the thoughts you have about yourself. They are not the other person's thoughts. Remember, you are the one thinking those thoughts."

If we look for the best in a man, it makes sense that we will bring out the best. If we judge him, we'll never discover what sets him apart from the others; we'll only see his flaws.

To be in a relationship involves taking a risk. It might require looking at ourselves first and discovering we need to make a few changes; it requires being open and receptive to new experiences; it requires letting go of your attachments to past relationships and, most importantly, not comparing him to a last love or an imagined ideal man. We need to truly experience him, as we need him to truly experience us.

**Hang On to Your Power**

Sometimes in a new relationship, when it's obvious your man loves being with you, but is not eagerly wanting to make a commitment, you start to feel the power you had at the beginning of your relationship slowly start to diminish. This is a good time to step back, create more space in your relationship by generating more excitement in your own life and to bring the spark back in your relationship. A few suggestions to reclaim your personal power:

> ➤ Hang out with friends who share your interests and your values.
> ➤ Get out of your comfort zone—be spontaneous and "in the moment."
> ➤ Pursue your own interests and hobbies; explore your creativity.

- ➢ Volunteer; get involved in meaningful projects; establish new friendships.
- ➢ Work out. Try aerobics, weight training, running, yoga, Pilates, tai chi, etc.
- ➢ Meditate: Mentally and physically enriching

If you've been on a dating frenzy without much success, stop the madness—take a break. Return to activities that bring you joy; for instance, have a spa day or a girlfriends' weekend. Get out of town. Finish a project, or resurrect a long-held goal you previously shelved. Join a group who share similar interests, such as hiking, walking, tennis or golf. This not only will boost your confidence, but it will give you a renewed sense of self, making you want to get back into dating. And most important, always have something that you can look forward to in the future, whether it is a vacation, a shopping trip, a theater production, entertaining friends, a weekend getaway, or whatever lights up your life.

**Falling into the Wrong Kinds of Relationships**

Author Carol Cassell says in *Swept Away*, "We exchange the brief moments of euphoria we get when we fall in love for long hours of depression, anger, and hostility when an encounter doesn't follow the fictitious course we've plotted."

Some women keep attracting the wrong kinds of relationships into their lives. They do not believe they can have the man they truly desire, instead, they settle for the one who pays them attention. Desperation often plays a part if it has been a while since their last relationship, making them vulnerable and more apt to lower their standards. With a healthier self image, they would automatically raise the bar and start making better choices in the types of men they let into their lives.

"Whatever relationships you have attracted into your life at any given time are the relationships you need to be in at that time. Whenever those dynamics change, there are others waiting to enter your life and meet the person you are becoming."

Deepak Chopra

### Attracting the Perfect Right Partner

*Chemistry happens when two hearts spontaneously connect,*
*without reason.*
*When we let our guard down and are being ourselves.*

Some ladies swear by writing out in detail the particulars of their ideal man or doing a vision board—collecting pictures of all the things they want and sticking them on a board to look at frequently.

I once knew a gal who would set her table for two, complete with candles and two glasses of wine. Of course, she'd end up drinking both glasses, but she eventually found her mate. I imagine it was a sobering experience.

## What Makes Men Fall in Love?

On Yahoo!Health, in an article provided by *Men'sHealth*, David Zinczenko posted: "Many men say they like a woman who's immersed in something else other than the relationship—be it her work or her sport, or whatever her 'thing' is. Why? The passion she shows for something else confirms her inherent goodness, her personal drive, her independence. All pluses in the woman we're hoping to spend a few decades with." Another attractive quality Zinczenko points out is "the strut":

"It's that attitude, that sassiness, that confidence, that charisma, that charm that shows she can be a little bold and a little daring.

. . . in certain aspects of relationships, men want women who have the strut. Men want to be with women who challenge them, who push them, and who take the lead some of the times. And that's as true in the bedroom as it is in planning their next weekend getaway.

127

. . . that gentle guidance—helping men make decisions without being harsh or judgmental. Women who can help steer us, without aggressively grabbing the wheel, are the most treasured copilots."

## Chapter 7

## Finding Our Passion

*Passion: A head—heart connection*
*when we are inspired and living "in the moment".*

We can get in touch with our passion by consistently following our interests—the activities to which we are naturally drawn, and by being keenly aware of our innate talents.

> ➢ What gives you goose bumps?
> ➢ What do you consistently daydream about?
> ➢ What do others tell you you'd be good at doing?

➤ What interests or hobbies cause you to lose track of time?
➤ What activities/hobbies did you love as a child?
➤ What would you do if you knew you couldn't fail?
➤ What keeps showing up in your life?
➤ What do you excel at?
➤ What activities make you feel good about yourself?
➤ What makes you feel alive?
➤ What do you feel most proud of?

Jeff Herring, a licensed marriage and family therapist in Tallahassee, Florida, once wrote:

"You may have heard this story, but it's worth repeating:

This kid came home from school one day, slammed his school books down on the table, ran upstairs, slammed the door, and broke down and cried. It was his tenth-grade year. His mother came in and said, "Son, what's wrong?" He said, "I got cut. I didn't make the team. They said I was too small."

With incredible wisdom, the mother said, "Son, it's not the size of the person in the game; it's the size of the game in the person." She left.

It clicked. In a huge way. Like nothing ever had before.

The next morning, he got up at 4:30 a.m. and started practicing—every morning, every evening, every day, every week, every month, relentless, nonstop.

His fight had been ignited, and he would not be denied. Through the snow, rain, sleet, ice, wind, and hail, he kept practicing, and he gave up movies and things that he had done before. The fight kept getting bigger. And bigger. And bigger.

The next year he made the team. His name? Michael Jordan. "

## Keep Growing and Expanding

If you want to know what thoughts you've been thinking and the choices you've been making pay attention to the results that consistently show up in your life. Good news! You can easily change your results by changing your thoughts and by changing your actions. Even the smallest shift can bring about a radically different result.

If our intention is to live a purposeful life, the result will be a healthy, happy, loving and prosperous existence. If we chase after it, it will continue to elude us. This reminds me of a gift I once received, with the following inscription:

> *Happiness is like a butterfly. The more you chase it,*
> *the more it will elude you, but if you turn your attention*
> *to other things, it will come and softly sit on your shoulder.*

We are happiest when we surround ourselves with those we love and who love us, when we are financially secure, when we are involved in activities that challenge us and help us to grow, when we feel peace within and with the world, and when we can be of service to others.

## Chapter 8

## Remembering What's Important

Back in 1994, Paul Glick, who was dying of cancer, appeared on *The Oprah Winfrey Show.* I was fascinated by what he had to say.

- Learn to be satisfied with what is happening in the present moment.
- Regrets are washed away with acceptance.
- Don't waste time on things that are not important.
- Learn to be satisfied with your life; do things to make it satisfactory.

- Find possibilities far beyond.
- In order for anybody to change, he or she has to be a self-observer.
- Recognize your attachments; there is no permanence in anything. Practice nonattachment.
- Everything is an illusion.
- Meditation is the way to get into the cracks between our thoughts. Practice, over time, gives us more access to ourselves.
- Absorb as much as you can every day.

It's our willingness to be open to what's next that allows our lives to transform.

It's insanity to believe that if we keep doing the same thing, we'll get a different result. Sometimes we need to question why we believe certain things, especially when we keep sabotaging what we say we want. Once we change our perception—changing from the inside out—things begin to change.

## Chapter 9

## There's the Life You Planned, and Then There's What Comes Next

No way did I ever think I'd be single again after marrying the man who vowed, as I vowed, to share the rest of our lives together. But as we all know, things change, people change, and here I am dating again—a little wiser and a little more prepared (six years after a divorce) to try again.

Marriage was a great learning experience for me—mostly in hindsight, looking back and seeing what I would have done differently. I determined that communication and putting each other first was the glue—the most important aspects of keeping a marriage intact. If we both tell each other what's right (what we love and appreciate) and what's wrong (what is not working and what needs to be discussed), we can fine-tune and sort it out along the way. If we don't, a gap begins to appear in the relationship, and it keeps getting wider and wider. Before we know it, quietness looms like an elephant in the room, and no matter how many times we ask, "Is there anything wrong?" the deeper truth is never revealed and therefore never discussed or resolved so that we can move forward. We started out with the right mind-set: "I will do everything within my power to make you happy." Because there was such a strong, magnetic, karmic connection from the outset and the ease in which our lives fell into place, we seemed destined to be mates for life. Divine Spirit had other plans.

Even though I had been single for many years prior to getting married, the transition back to living single again was difficult at first, perhaps more so because of my resistance. I had loved coming home to someone greeting me with a hug; having someone to make plans with, to laugh with, and to play with. Once I accepted my new status, it became an adventure. One in which I get to choose exactly how to play it going forward to live a life well lived.

I believe certain people come into our lives when they are most needed and point us in the right direction. One of those people was my friend Karen, with whom I had an instant connection during a volunteer stint. She not only was interesting and fun, but she also was spiritual and led me to the Center for Spiritual Living in Palm Desert. I didn't realize it until then that spirituality was an important part that had been missing in my life. I spent the first year taking as many classes as I could fit in, met new friends, and eventually evolved to a more grounded state.

As for my dating life . . . I am still in the process. The first year after my husband and I went our separate ways, I had no interest in jumping back into the dating scene. Gradually, a few men trickled into my life while attending seminars; through friends; at a local happy hour bar, local restaurant, or dance venue; and a few ex-boyfriends resurfaced. No sparks—until this past summer, when I was in Vancouver, British Columbia, visiting family and friends, and I happened to reconnect with a boyfriend I had dated in my twenties. Amazingly, our paths keep crossing about every decade. This tells me we have more to learn.

I could easily have left this book in my desk drawer, with all its interesting stories waiting to be told, but an inner voice urged me to resurrect it and get it out into the world. My desire to inspire other women to believe in true love beyond forty still exists. Enjoy!

## The Best Is Yet to Come!

# References

Behrendt, Greg & Tuccillo, Liz — *He's Just Not That Into You (Simon Spotlight Entertainment, Div. of Simon & Schuster, Inc. 2004)*

Denise, Jan — *Inside Relationships Newspaper Column,* Release Date: April 28, 2006

Downs, Maggie — Tips for Dating over Fifty *The Desert Sun newspaper,* Palm Springs, California, dated Nov. 27, 2005

Downs, Maggie — Tips for Dating at Any Age *The Desert Sun* newspaper, Palm Springs, California, dated Nov. 27, 2005

Gray, John, Ph. D. — *Men Are from Mars, Women Are from Venus, (NY HarperCollins, 1ˢᵗ edition, Apr. 23, 1993)*

Hanover, Donna — *My Boyfriend's Back*, (A Plume Book, Penguin Group Dec 27, 2005)

Shreve, Anita

*A Wedding in December*, (Little Brown & Co., 1st edition Oct. 10, 2005)

Vanzant, Iyanla

*In the Meantime . . . Finding Yourself & the Love you Want, (NY Simon & Schuster 1998, Touchstone First Fireside edition Sept. 14, 1999)*

Viscott, David, M.D.

Risking, (NY Simon & Schuster First Edition edition, Jan 15, 1978)

Zinczenko, David

Yahoo! Health *Men's Health* article, posted "What Makes Men Fall in Love?", Mar. 15, 2007 http://health.yahoo.com/experts/menlovesex/24834/what-makes-men-fall-in-love

CPSIA information can be obtained at www.ICGtesting.com
Printed in the USA
BVOW031549261012

303983BV00003B/1/P